EMILY JACKMAN • PAUL JACKMAN • ERIC JACKMAN • MAURISSA JENNINGS •
VANESSA JONES • WILLIAM R. JONES • MICHAEL JONES • DOUGLAS KANE • DAEW
OAN KAUFMAN • DAVID N. KAY • ROSS KEARNS • PATRICK KEETLEY • J. ANDREW KELLER • COLLEN KELLY
ELIZABETH KELLY • KACI KEPFERLE • STEVEN KNIGHT • MEAGHAN KROENER • MARISA KURTZMAN
EE LAM • PALMER LANE • PAUL LANGLAND • MANUEL LAUZURIQUE • GEOFFREY LAWSON • DOUG B. LEE • JOHN LENKIN
CORNELIUS IVES LISTER JR. • GREGORY LOMAN • JEFFREY LOMAN • MICHELLE LOPEZ-ORSINI • JOHNNY MAAS
GLENN MACCULLOUGH • JEREMY MACK • BEN MADDOX • LEAH MALITO • W. CLARK MANNING • YOLANDA MARINA
ERRY MARSHALL • LESLIE E. MASON • NASIR MASOOD • LISA MATEY • WAMBAA MATHU • ROBERT MCCLURE
FIONA E. MUELKEN • GABRIELLE M. MUISE • ABDUL MUZIKIR • JOHN NAHRA • JOHN N. NAMMACK • PATRICK NELSON
MATT NEUMANN • MATT C. NEWBURN • SEAN NOHELTY • JOHN J. NOLIS • STEVEN K. NOSE • HAYES NUSS
BRIAN O'LOONEY • MATTHEW M. OSSOLINSKI • JENNIFER PALOSKI • STEVE PAYNE • ROLAND O. PEPIN
THERESA PETRAMALE • STACEY PHILLIPS • TODD S. PHILLIPS • JOEL PIDEL • PIER D. PIERANDOREI • JULIA PILIPOVICH
CHRIS PIZZI • MATTHEW POE • LUIS G. PONS • RHIANNON PORTER • WILLIAM POULOS • JUAN PRIETO • LISA Y. QUINLIN
AMES RAMSEY • DONNA RENDELMAN • JOSEPH RAPAZZO • PETER REIGER • JON A. REINHARD • DIANA S. REUTER
OHNATHAN RICH • ARIANE RISTO • JON ERIC RITLAND • NOEMI B. RIVIERA • KIMBERLY A. ROLLINGS • STEPHEN M. SAFF
PEDRO SALES • CHRISTOPHER SALVADORE • MUHAMMADALI SAMI • BRUCE W. SANFORD • DAVID M. SCHWARZ
EFFERY SCOTT • ELIZABETH T. SHEPARD • EVAN G. SIEGEL • KIMBERLY P. SIMONS • BJORN SLATE • MARY K SLEVIN
SANDRA SMART • KEN D. SMITH • TIMOTHY SO • JESSICA SOFFER • SEAN STADLER • DAVID J. STASS • ZACHARY STEWART
THOMAS J. STODGHILL • STEPHEN STRASSER • MIKE SUTTON • MICHAEL SWARTZ • HEATHER TARNER • SHALINI TANEJA
BARRIE TEACH • KEN TERZIAN • JEFFERSON B. THOMAS • ERIK THOMPSON • KENT TITTLE • ROLAND TOMASSO
AMES M. VANDERPUTTE • JEFF VANHOUTEN • CATHERINE VISEN • PHILLIP WAGNER • DOUGLAS WARD
MAGDA WESTERHOUT • WILLIAM WHITE • DANIELLE WILKENS • CRAIG P. WILLIAMS • JEFFREY WILSON • ALEX J. WITKO
MARK F. WOUTERS • HUGH XU • JOY YODER • RICHARD ZAMBITO • MOIGAN ZARE • JON G. ZUBILLER • LAUREN F. ZUZACK

David M. Schwarz Architects

2002–2007

David M. Schwarz Architects

BY ROBERT L. MILLER

WITH A PREFACE

BY DAVID M. SCHWARZ

© Copyright 2008 by:
David M. Schwarz Architects
1707 L Street, NW, Suite 400
Washington, DC 20036
Tel (202) 862-0777
www.dmsas.com

Grayson Publishing
James G. Trulove, Publisher
1250 28th Street, NW
Washington, DC 20007
Tel (202) 257-5959
jtrulove@aol.com

Hardcover ISBN: 978-0-9679143-3-6
Softcover ISBN: 978-0-9679143-5-0

Printed in China

First Printing: 2008

1 2 3 4 5 6 7

The author and publisher join with David Schwarz Architects in dedicating this book to the firm's clients throughout 30 years, in gratitude for their role in supporting architecture and the built environment through this firm's works and ideas, with added thanks to the artists, artisans and craftsmen who have contributed to the success of the firm's projects.

Contents

Preface

DAVID M. SCHWARZ

Publication of this book marks the thirtieth anniversary of David M. Schwarz Architects. It is hard to understand our firm and its work without knowing a little of my personal history. There are two little known and never connected facts that have gone into forging our firm, and caused us to practice architecture and planning as we do. First, I was born and spent my early formative years in Los Angeles, about which Reyner Banham wrote a famous and influential book published in 1971. It glorified much of what I hated about my Los Angeles childhood: celebrating the automobile, lauding suburbanization, and glorifying the lack of traditional urban fabric via the breakup and isolation of disparate communities. Second, in 1978 the District of Columbia passed the most sweeping historic preservation law ever passed by any jurisdiction up to that point, and Congress passed the Tax Reform Act of 1976, which included tax credits for historic preservation development projects. Neither of these events alone would have caused me to take the direction I have, but the two combined were formative to my views on how to build, and more particularly, how to build places for people.

I grew up in what at the time was a backwater of the not yet arrived, or already past their prime, movie stars: the likes of Buddy Ebsen (after *Davy Crockett* and before Jed Clampett), Jayne Mansfield (after *The Girl Can't Help It* but before her encounter with the tiger), Steve McQueen (after *The Great Escape* but before his untimely death) and Fess Parker (after everything). An accident of fate (or city planning) caused this little street called Hutton Drive to actually be

the only piece of L. A. with a Beverly Hills post office address, what became the now famous 90210. At the time, the only road to our family home on Hutton Drive was through Beverly Hills, and so the postman had to be a Beverly Hills postman. This made it a perfect place for those who craved but could not afford the "right" post office. It was quite literally the end (or the beginning) of the line. My father chose it because he fantasized it a great place to raise children. One could have horses, go hiking or generally lead that good, outdoor life so celebrated, but which held absolutely no interest for me.

The downside was that, without a driver's license, I was shackled to my street. There was no viable way for a non-driving kid to go anywhere. As was true of so many other post-World War II suburban neighborhoods, there were no sidewalks, no bike paths, no public transportation and, as the major arterial was a very busy route to and from "the valley", biking was not an option. School was in the flats. Home was in the hills. A yawning gulf existed between the two. The only way to get anywhere was to be chauffeured by "mom" or someone else's mom. It left very little independence for a kid who craved it.

I first read *Los Angeles: The Architecture of Four Ecologies*, by Reyner Banham, while I was in architecture school. It caused me to reflect on my childhood. It glorified the freedom brought by the automobile and celebrated a walking free world. It struck me as a highly intellectualized look at what was in fact a physically, socially and culturally marooned world: the world in which I

had grown up, and a world of which I was not particularly fond. It made me wonder and worry about where we, as a society, were headed. It put a big question mark over much of what I was learning in school.

I was educated in architecture in the early 1970's, at the end of the "International School" modernist era. My professors were Jim Sterling, Charles Moore, Sam Davis, Lou Brody, Charles Gwathmey and Peter Eisenman. Like the rest of my class, I graduated into the world with modernist training and a modernist outlook on the world. As I moved into the real world, it was via working for Charles Moore, Paul Rudolph and Edward Larabee Barnes.

After my required apprenticeship, I decided to move from New York to Washington, D.C. to open my own firm. Washington was a city at the beginning of a period of great growth, which struck me as being a time of great architectural opportunity as well. Shortly after arriving, the District passed its groundbreaking historic preservation law, and Congress passed a tax reform act with significant incentives for historic preservation. Washington was then a city of lawyers always looking for a way to shelter their income. This created a niche business for us and other young firms: restoring historic structures and working in historic districts.

We began studying individual historic buildings, as well as entire historic districts, and learned a great deal about how and why cities had been built as they had been and what made them successfully work now. D.C. was an urban laboratory for us. We began to understand how streetscapes and neighborhoods are knit together. The principles we discovered were far from the modernist approach I had learned in school. I had to completely relearn how to look at and experience buildings, neighborhoods and cities.

Our firm established a series of guidelines for rehabilitating and reusing historic structures and, more importantly, we developed a set of categories for ourselves to help define the task at hand. We concluded that each project fell into one of three categories: museum-quality preservation; adaptive reuse; or neighborhood preservation. It was important in our practice to understand into which of these categories each project fell. This gave us a greater understanding of how to proceed.

Without realizing it, we also were developing an attitude as well as an implicit set of guidelines for our new town planning and architecture projects. What we had called museum-quality preservation became the paradigm for important civic object buildings such as Bass Hall or the Town Hall in Southlake. Adaptive reuse became our guide for understanding how to create fabric buildings in existing contexts, as well as in our new town planning projects. And neighborhood preservation became neighborhood creation as we set out to make new places that had the richness and complexity of the pre-war American town or city. Our work in Washington became a template for place-making for the various neighborhoods and contexts in which we have built.

Obviously, every street, neighborhood, town and city is somewhat different, so our

first steps have always been to understand the context in which we plan or build. The methodology here is very similar to the one we first learned while trying to understand the streetscapes and neighborhoods of Washington, D.C.

Without a great deal of forethought or planning, we developed a view of ourselves as populist architects, and began to define ourselves as neo-eclectics, as our goal became to make places for people, created out of a fabric that was familiar and easy to understand. We have always wanted to make places that "feel good" rather than "think good". We have always believed in an emotional rather than an intellectual attachment to place. We have always wanted to create places that further community and foster a sense of pride, both from the people who commission them as well as those who use them, either actively or passively. We grew to appreciate what made pre-World War II communities so wonderful, and to disdain that which Banham so incorrectly embraced in his book, which in our view only furthered the wasteful suburbanization and urban anomie of the United States.

Time has demonstrated that our developed society can no longer embrace the wasteful practices of the Twentieth Century. Land is not an endless commodity. Buildings should not be disposable. Human capital and time are not infinite. Preservation and conservation are becoming a necessity rather than the purview of a rarified few. Our built environment must reflect these principles if we are going to succeed. Unlike the Twentieth Century, ours is fast becoming an era of limitation and conservation: of

energy, of resources and of manpower. We need new models of urban design, rejecting the attitudes and principles of the previous half century, a time of thoughtless excess and overweening hubris.

The notion that there is anything "new" about New Urbanism is a highly problematic point of view. Current urbanism is no different from old urbanism. The only difference is that we are designing for vehicles with hundreds of "horsepower" rather than somewhere between one and four. Current "horsepower" simply requires larger roads and larger "stables".

The notion of "new" has an over-exalted position in our world today. Beginning with the theories of the International School, it became synonymous with rejection, destruction, and ultimately ignorance of the past. In wholly embracing the new, we risk missing that which is good and relevant about how we came to be whom and what we are today. We at David M. Schwarz Architects therefore have chosen to carefully examine urban and community history and traditions, and carry forward those that we believe are still important and relevant. These are the foundations upon which we have built this practice. Much as the first "Eclectics" re-fabricated their traditions in a new light to bring something new and fresh to their world, so have we. We have come to understand that in timelessness there is undying relevance. Rather than rejecting and destroying our history and traditions, we can carry forward and reinvent, adding a richness and vitality to how we look at our world today.

Modern Populist

ROBERT L. MILLER

10 David Schwarz's long-term enterprise ("cause" is a word he would find immodest) is to devise ways in which modern architecture can restore popular, urban civility to an American environment that, even within city limits, is pervasively suburbanized.

Schwarz is one of many architects and planners interested in urbanizing suburbia, not a few of whom see this as the opportunity of the age. More than most, however, he combines a practical understanding of real suburban projects with a demanding standard for designing them as real architecture. Schwarz nicely overcomes both the distractions of ideology and the comforts of superficiality. He is much more likely to be found trying to make something better out of a planned strip shopping center or a downtown parking lot than debating a universal zoning code, and he lets others preach the true faith of classicism or the mores of Elm Street. At the same time, a Schwarz riff on neoclassicism begins with a thorough understanding of how Scamozzi proportioned an Ionic order, thoughtfully adjusted to the properties of EIFS synthetic stucco or Indiana limestone. Uncondescending and deceptively artless-looking, the Schwarz firm's urban/suburban interventions are clearly based on dogged study of older retail buildings, with details worked out to the last brick.

As the five years of built projects shown in this volume demonstrate, this is architects' architecture, friendlier to some ideologies than others but in the end free from cant, old or new. The possibilities of computer design and fabrication, experimental materials, "green" or sustainable or high-performance criteria are at work in many of these projects, but usually behind the scenes. Never ironic (but rarely humorless), this architecture holds to the Vitruvian basics: accommodating people in the broadest sense, performing physically over time, and giving something of beauty and enjoyment back to a place and its populace.

By being "only" architectural and not requiring further explanation, the work is, paradoxically perhaps, unusually understandable to people in general. Even the label-resistant Schwarz is willing to call this work populist.

In politics, where the word has a traceable history, the meanings of populism have shifted from decade to decade. A bare definition—an appeal to the needs and desires of common people, often in opposition to an elite—seems clear enough. And yet it has been applied to movements across the political spectrum. Its application to architecture invites a moment's reflection.

Twentieth-century modernist architects often considered themselves populists by definition, whether or not they used the word. Many embraced socialism, which encouraged professionals to reject the hierarchies and hothouse aesthetics of the old elites and work toward air, green space, and affordable housing for all, trusting that both a social and aesthetic utopia would follow. Many also accepted the corollary that an architecture for the people should derive from the climate-sensitive, site-specific buildings that common people build for themselves in, for example, rural Italy or Morocco, modified to suit the imperatives of modern technology and mass production.

How these ideas helped achieve better housing for millions of people and helped create beautiful modernist buildings, and yet proved disastrous as a guide for making an urban public realm that people could wholeheartedly endorse, is a story too often told to bear repeating here.

It may be enough to note that the masses living in authentic, sun-drenched austerity did not necessarily want to continue living that way in a developed society. Architecture, as realized in building, is a stubbornly expensive enterprise that often requires the involvement of elites, public or private, visionary or reactionary, through the ages. Nevertheless, common people often embrace and enjoy the resulting gorgeousness. Almost everyone loves (although few can now afford) Paris, an imperial capital that ruthlessly displaced common people, built miles of absurdly hierarchical neo-Renaissance boulevards, stressed fine arts and unfamiliar food among its elitist offerings, and still outdraws every purpose-built mass attraction.

David Schwarz began architecture school at a special time and place, where the populist assumptions of modernism were being tested both intellectually and on the ground. As New Haven underwent a heroic modernist remaking as a freeway-enabled adjunct to its own suburbs, a conflicting realization was dawning there and elsewhere: that people cared deeply about the loss of their old urban experience. The 1965 issue of the Yale School of Architecture journal *Perspecta*, edited by the school's current dean, Robert A. M. Stern, remains a touchstone of that era. It includes Vincent Scully's essay on the "suburban doldrums" of both Bauhaus and home-grown American modernism in the late 1930s and '40s; Charles Moore's "You Have to Pay for the Public Life," which finds Disneyland the best civic environment in California; and a version of Robert Venturi's *Complexity and Contradiction in Architecture*, later much misread but then simply a "gentle

manifesto" for modern architecture open to context, pop culture, old urbanism, symbol, and ornament. Elsewhere, historic preservation had become a gut issue for American architecture, following the destruction of New York's Pennsylvania Station the year before. Jane Jacobs' *The Death and Life of Great American Cities*, in 1961, had signaled a new balance of power between neighborhood preservation and urban renewal. While the focus of these years was on a revived civic populism, the theme of individual populism, as symbolized by the rediscovery of "punched," operable windows and the ordinary experiential values catalogued in Christopher Alexander's *A Pattern Language*, gained prominence a little later in the 1970s.

All these people and ideas would come together in David Schwarz's practice and teaching career, and many would reappear later in his stewardship of the Vincent Scully Prize of the National Building Museum.

Today at David M. Schwarz Architects, the architects apply populist ideas at three scales. There is that *civic* dimension, a sense of connection to the city as a whole and, usually, a multi-block context, explored in a master plan. Related to this is what can be called a *street* dimension, a commitment to what happens where

the building meets the sidewalk and how pedestrians experience this. And there is an *individual* dimension—mostly, but not exclusively, indoors—for those who actively use the facility, both visitors and day-to-day inhabitants.

Schwarz and some of his present colleagues were modernist-trained young architects at the point in the late 1970s when historic preservation changed from a geriatric hobby to a popular movement—a tool, sometimes the only one available, with which ordinary citizens could affect urban design. Equipped with academic ideas about the contemporaneity of history, Schwarz learned a great deal in Washington, D.C., about how mastering architecture's past could fulfill the demands of a tradition-oriented market, disarm neighbors resisting change, and satisfy bureaucratic agendas. A corollary lesson involved the imperative of master planning beyond one's own project, not least as a way of getting ahead of the political curve.

The firm's emphasis on preserving or creating a popular civic presence and a holistic plan, including sustainable use of resources and other less visible public goals, characterizes most of the projects on these pages. Many relate to an existing urban context, including high-profile examples—the Cook Children's Medical

12 Center addition and Tarrant County Family Law Center in Fort Worth; the Schermerhorn Symphony Center in Nashville; and the Chapman Cultural Center in Spartanburg, South Carolina—that pursue explicit civic, popular agendas. Others—especially the Texas mixed-use projects, which range in scale from a five-block neighborhood to a small city center—largely create their own urban context, informed by close observation of local styles and vernaculars.

The idea of giving modern architecture a public street presence is often honored in design criteria but surprisingly elusive in practice. Preservation, again, helped re-educate these modern architects. They learned that buildings do not always need to give literal, physical access from the street in order to carry on a public dialogue, through street-level windows, sheltering devices, street furniture, and especially detail and ornament. Buildings like the imaginatively (and economically) ornamented Bank One, and even more so the simple but infinitely varied commercial fronts of Southlake's Grand Avenue, Parker Square, Frisco Square, and Firewheel Town Center, attract and reward pedestrians with orchestrated wayfinding cues, color and material changes, geometric ornament, site-specific symbols, and glimpses through glass.

With work such as the city-park gates of the Dr Pepper Ballpark concourse; the big, open arches of the Beringer winery; and the monumentalized storefront of the Sid Richardson Museum, these architects consistently escape the blankly prismatic or bunker-like ground plane of many contemporary buildings, to provide visual openness and an understandable way to enter. Finally, and not incidentally, they recognize that many real-world pedestrians begin and end their trips as motorists. Although most of these projects conceal or separate parking, they provide ample amounts of it, integrate it in balance with buildings and landscape, and make it easy to navigate by vehicle or on foot.

Windows are a source of pride with this firm and a key to Schwarz's recipe for interiors that provide people with positive, supportive experiences. While employing the modernist window wall or room-size skylight wherever appropriate, these architects emphasize the large "French" casement window and, especially, the oversize double-hung window combinations common in the early 20th century, all in today's high-performance versions. The presence of individual windows, together with familiar room shapes and details, is of particular importance in the Fort Worth projects that serve children and families in stressful

isolation: the new Cook Children's Medical Center intensive-care wing and the Tarrant County Family Law Center. But tall, generous windows also make a difference to the ballet instructors at the Chapman Cultural Center and the bond traders at the Bank One Building. More than any other element they lend nobility to plain loft spaces, while visually and symbolically reconnecting the individual and the city.

Windows in the firm's public interiors are normally part of a scale-giving order, often derived from Beaux-Arts classicism: a spare but thoughtful system of material and ornament that lends a sense of orientation, security, and implicit dignity. Perhaps the most wide-ranging illustration here is the Schermerhorn Symphony Center. Instead of wrapping a sculptural bunker around its concert hall, Schermerhorn, a center in more than name, makes each major ancillary public space a room with it's own access to natural light and, in many cases, its own presence on the building exterior.

One can admire Schwarz's latter-day try at a modern architecture for the people—based on civic responsibility, a pedestrian street experience, and the dignity of the individual patient, worker, or visitor—and still ask why the result almost always ends up looking like an old building. He would reply, I think, that in most cases it needn't. Another dimension of the firm's populism is its willingness to defer to clients in matters of style. The firm not only embraces eclecticism and "the style for the job" (once practiced by many historicists as well as modernists like Eero Saarinen), but also presents clients with alternate designs in alternate styles. Given the firm's reputation and clientele, it may be slightly disingenuous for Schwarz to explain his work on the basis that his clients rarely choose the modern alternative. However, one should not quickly dismiss Schwarz's claim to be a modern architect, or ignore the firm's designs that are explicitly modern in whole or part.

On inspection, it seems true that the firm employs history less for 19th-century romance than for 21st-century function. A glance through this book reveals forms and images that the architects clearly chose to enhance existing contexts, or to appeal to established commercial or residential markets. Elsewhere, historically based forms—such as the Bank One Building's double-hung windows, or the gypsum-board coffers in the Spartanburg theater—may simply do a given job better than any high-tech alternative. Given American society's cultural multiplicity, and the reality of American building technology, these 60- to 100-year-old forms are arguably full of relevance and value. Schwarz's intellectually courageous experiment is to take architectural fashion out of the equation and place new and old forms and images in the available repertoire of solutions.

That said, it appears that the firm's interests in populism, civic responsibility, pedestrian-friendly urbanism, and American art and context have led its design preferences in the same general direction. So have its studies of the Washington, D.C., and Dallas-Fort Worth metropolitan areas and their histories of architecture and urbanism. The coincidental theme in much of the work shown here is the mainstream architecture of the two Roosevelt administrations, with their common interest in a popular, civic role for design, and their common belief in a civilized, progressive French-taught neoclassicism as an alternative to revolutionary modernism.

The Tarrant County Family Law Center and the Schermerhorn Symphony Center owe the most to the progressive, City Beautiful sensibility of Theodore Roosevelt and architectural advisors, although the axial clarity of Beaux-Arts planning appears in many Schwarz projects. The Franklin Roosevelt era of Art Deco, Art Moderne, and the Works Project Administration is explicit in the National Cowgirl Museum, a valentine to the Texas Deco of the adjacent Will Rodgers Center. In the town center projects, where the architects often reconstitute a visually plausible, decades-long history, the cornices of the 1910s alternate with the pinnacles and streamlines of the 1930s, all simplified in the way of small-town builders everywhere. The historic references are lightly applied, and the ornament is freshly reinvented with symbols specific to the project, although with the sense that everything is firmly rooted in some accurately measured original.

The domestic and smaller-scale projects included here have less to do, appropriately, with civic presence and purpose, but they share related qualities of generosity and environmental balance. The Mediterranean-flavored wineries, the Hawken School athletic facility with its whiff of polo ponies, and the shingled New England summer house all seem at first to offer a little high-calorie postmodern romance, but a close look reveals an armature of 21st-century rationality. The Dr Pepper Ballpark, a civic structure with a light, almost residential character, does encourage sustained daydreams of summer, possibly influenced by the firm's earlier work on a more specifically fantastic ballfield for Walt Disney World in Florida.

14 The list of architectural sources and heroes imbedded in these designs is a long one, from H.H. Richardson and Julia Morgan to the Austrian and Czech designers who often outdid the French in the international search for a modern neoclassicism. A list of the artistic influences is even farther beyond our scope here, ranging from Schwarz's own extensive collection of American graphic and applied art of the 1920s, '30s, and '40s, through the anti-ironic treatment of popular culture that continues from Andy Warhol through Jeff Koons and later contemporaries.

If one had to choose only one piece of cultural context for this latest work of David Schwarz, it might be the career of the transplanted French academic Paul Phillipe Cret (1876-1945). Working primarily in Philadelphia, Texas, and Washington, D.C., Cret bridged from Beaux-Arts to Moderne, and influenced later modern and postmodern generations as a teacher and mentor of Louis Kahn.

Theodore Roosevelt himself inaugurated Cret's 1910 headquarters for the Organization of American States, then known as the Pan American Union. A rich but well-integrated combination of multicultural art and landscape with an exemplary Beaux-Arts building, this is an early exemplar of Schwarz's belief that the reasonableness of classicism can make environments warm, meaningful, and accessible. In the early 1930s, with such designs as the Folger Shakespeare Library, the Federal Reserve headquarters, and Fort Worth's United States Post Office and Courthouse, Cret helped transform the fashionable sleekness of Art Deco into a popular civic language that endured the Depression. The ideas of these buildings—especially the achievement of classical organization with pared-down classical detail, and the graceful incorporation of modern materials and place-specific art and ornament—are precursors of Schwarz's approach. Finally, while it may not be literally true that Cret translated Franklin Roosevelt's napkin sketch into the design of the original Bethesda Naval Hospital, Cret devoted self-effacing creative energy to public commissions for power plants, bridges, exhibition buildings, and cemeteries, like Schwarz accommodating every kind of client.

Following Cret's humanist tradition, Schwarz sees in the extant 20th-century city a set of valuable, flexible architectural principles and tools that remain applicable to human needs—needs that, in the midst of technological and political change, remain remarkably constant. There are problems to be solved; no need to invent new ones for the sake of design. These solutions, while old, have been successfully reinvented, updated, and retrofitted many times and applied by geniuses and journeymen alike. The message of the elegant, pragmatic projects shown here is that modernism is fine when it works, and whatever else works ought to be welcome, too, especially if one believes that the original, populist ideals of modern architecture deserve to be realized.

Robert L. Miller, FAIA, is an architect, writer, and consultant who lives and works in Washington, D.C.

Projects

National Cowgirl Museum and Hall of Fame

FORT WORTH, TEXAS 2002

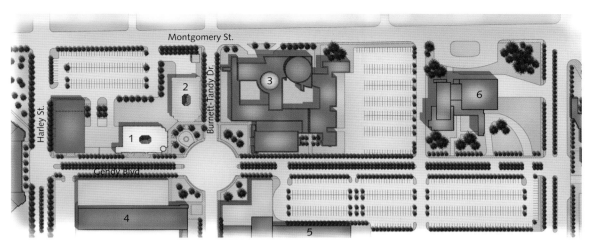

**Western Heritage Center
Master Plan, 2000**

1. National Cowgirl Museum
   & Hall of Fame
2. Future Cattle Raisers
   Museum
3. Science & History Museum
4. Livestock Barn
5. Amon Carter Exhibition Hall
6. Modern Art Museum

Montgomery St.

Burnett-Tandy Dr.

Harley St.

Gendy Blvd.

0 100 200 250

Dedicated to the women from Annie Oakley to Sandra Day O'Connor who exemplify the pioneer spirit of the West, the National Cowgirl Museum and Hall of Fame presents their history straight-forwardly, with a moving feminist sub-text (one learns, for instance, that women competed as equals with men in rodeo events before World War II), all tem-pered with gentle humor.

Its new building is similarly forthright in delivering the dignity, clarity, and rich-ness expected in a museum of history and culture, with a freshness not always present in such institutions.

Together with its famous art museums, the tree-shaded Fort Worth Cultural Dis-trict revolves around the eighty-five-acre Will Rogers Center. This mid-1930's, Moderne style campus has a 2,900-seat coliseum, auditorium, exhibit halls, are-nas, and barns that regularly host rodeo, livestock and horse shows. The National Cowgirl Museum faces the Will Rogers complex and takes formal cues from its architect Wyatt Cephas Hedrick, also the designer of Fort Worth's Texas and Pacific Terminal (1931) and other Texas Deco landmarks.

From the beginning, expansion oppor-tunities, including cooperative relation-ships with neighboring institutions, were a project goal. The architects met with

Opposite: Cast stone spandrels and terra cotta finials display the wild rose, symbolizing the western wom-an's mix of beauty and toughness. Sculpted parapet panel, by Montage Imagers of Fort Worth, depicts the motto "Always saddle your own horse."

stakeholders and led a public design charrette to develop a projected Western Heritage Center master plan, involving the Cowgirl Museum, the adjacent Fort Worth Museum of Science and History, and a proposed relocation of the Cattle Raisers Museum. A study of alternate sites and their relationship to the Will Rogers campus led to the current master plan, which orients the Cowgirl Museum toward a new plaza to be shared with a future, adjoining building.

An octagonal lantern with geometric stainless steel grilles crowns the muse-um's corner bay and marks this incipient plaza, with the stainless steel marquee and main entrance facing the plaza itself at ninety degrees to the street.

From the octagonal corner tower, rows of stepped-back, rocket-like brick piers define two-story bays of stacked case-ment windows beneath a tall cast-stone parapet. The decorative program includes stylized wild rose pinnacles in glazed terra cotta above each main pier, a wild rose bas-relief on each spandrel, and realistic sculptural vignettes across the parapet, including a depiction of "Always saddle your own horse." The mostly win-dowless street elevation centers on Rich-ard Haas's two-story, trompe-l'oeil mural from which cowgirls in grisaille gallop out toward the viewer. Rear elevations in syn-thetic stucco facilitate future expansion; here stainless steel letters spell COW-GIRL to guide approaching visitors.

In the course of planning this, the muse-um's first purpose-built home, client and

architects agreed on distinct galleries with an orientation to natural light, ver-sus a "black box" approach controlled entirely by the exhibit designer. The cowgirl story, combining Hollywood and rodeo flamboyance with everyday ranch life, invites a balance between theater and reality helping to create a more museum-like experience. The visi-tor experience here includes drama; it offers a rideable mechanical bronco and a rhinestoned dress-up photo studio, for instance. At the same time, there is a nice interplay when these interactive surprises occur in high-ceiling rooms with elegantly framed doorways and sunlight beyond.

The light, sensed from the first step into the entrance lobby, comes from the domed, forty-five foot tall Rotunda's clerestory windows above a two-story colonnade. The Rotunda is actually both rectangular and oval—an inten-tional reference to the rodeo ring, and to architecture's greatest equestrian inte-rior, Fischer von Erlach's Winter Riding School in Vienna.

Visually tamed by classical proportions, the Rotunda in detail is a stampede of streamline Moderne-inspired entabla-tures, reinvented column orders with carved horse heads and wild rose capi-tals, and a variety of masonry, metal, and electronic graphic devices that record the Hall of Fame inductees honored each year in this space. The Rotunda's French limestone floor and custom-designed mahogany doors and furnishings con-tinue in the lower-ceilinged main lobby.

17

18

Above: A bird's eye view rendering shows the proposed Cattle Raisers Museum adjacent to the Cowgirl Museum.

Right: West façade, at right of photo, faces parking and identifies museum with backlit, stainless steel letters on parapet: synthetic stucco construction here anticipates future expansion.

Above: Street view from Will Rogers Center shows Richard Haas mural at left, main entrance facing Western Heritage Center Plaza at right.

Between these two spaces, open twin stairways give access to the second floor. Intricate aluminum-and-bronze railings again display the wild rose, the badge of cowgirl grace and toughness seen on the exterior, and reappearing on column pedestals and above gallery portals.

Lobby, Rotunda and stairs provide a clear access route between the first floor's theater and temporary exhibits, and the second floor's suite of permanent display galleries. The gallery circuit returns visitors to the lobby and museum shop, with a chance to revisit the Rotunda and its memorials.

Inside and out, the flamboyance of Texas Deco and an unexpected programmatic and ornamental richness help make the National Cowgirl Museum and Hall of Fame a satisfying experience. Despite the cowgirl/cowboy emphasis on stubborn independence, it sets the stage for a larger, cooperative Western heritage complex and a closer relationship with the Will Rogers Center.

Above: Cowgirl Plaza, a horseshoe in plan, provides a forecourt for the Cowgirl Museum entry and a setting for future construction.

Opposite: Main entrance details evoke Moderne style of adjacent Will Rogers Center; spandrel panels between windows incorporate the museum's signature wild rose motif.

Following Pages: Richard Haas's trompe d'oeil mural creates a streetside identity for the museum and a photo opportunity for visitors.

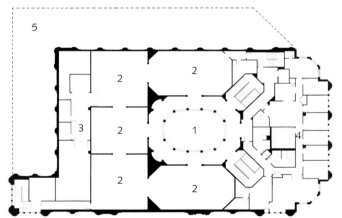

Second Floor Plan

1. Rotunda/Hall of Fame
2. Gallery (Permanent Exhibit)
3. Backstage
4. Temporary Admin Suite/ Future Gallery Space
5. Future Expansion Area

Above Left: From the ticketing desk visitors may walk straight ahead to the Rotunda's Hall of Fame displays and temporary shows, or proceed upstairs to permanent exhibits.

Above Right: Each second floor gallery opens to the natural light of the Rotunda.

Opposite: Within the light-filled Rotunda, interactive video screens and a band of stars recognize Cowgirl Hall of Fame inductees; some also appear in the parapet's LifeTile murals by Boston artist Rufus Butler Seder.

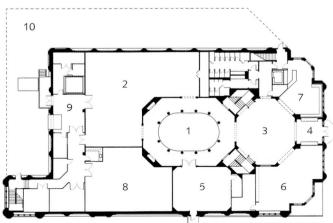

First Floor Plan

1. Rotunda/Hall of Fame
2. Flexible Exhibit Gallery
3. Lobby
4. Vestibule
5. Theater
6. Gift Shop
7. Food Service
8. Conservation
9. Loading
10. Future Expansion Area

0 10 20 40

Above and Left: Stair landing provides a close look at the Rotunda's horsehead-and-rose column capitals and the stylized wild rose (detail above) of the metal stair rail. Dark reveals in ceiling integrate linear air diffusers.

Above and Left: Order of columns designed specifically for the museum incorporates the horse and the wild rose. Rose medallions also appear on the column pedestals. LifeTile portrait shown depicts painter Georgia O'Keefe.

28

Left and Opposite: Galleries are designed as individual rooms. Dropped perimeter ceilings accommodate air distribution and track lighting; dark, raised ceilings incorporate lighting, video, and sound equipment. Left, a typical gallery highlights cowgirl fashions and video clips of women on horseback. Below left, ranch life exhibit includes interactive screens. Above opposite, Reel Cowgirls Gallery showcases movie and TV stars. Below opposite, visitors ride a mechanical bronco in front of a green screen, adding stock footage to make their own "rodeo" video.

Bank One Building

FORT WORTH, TEXAS   2002

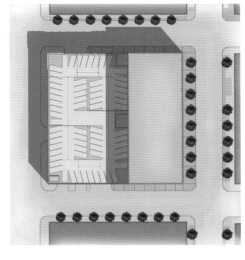

05 15 25

This twelve-story office building's presence on the street recalls early 20th century loft buildings and the Chicago School skyscrapers that preceded them, as well as historic Fort Worth towers like the Burke Burnett Building, with its exemplary base, shaft, and capital organization. Its decorative use of brick resonates with Texas history, from 1880's Ruskinian ornament through 1920's tapestry brick and Depression-era streamlining.

As so often happens with the firm, however, a careful look reveals a modern building of considerable originality. Its design explores what planar brick walls and conventional "punched" windows, too often relegated to rear elevations, can bring to a 21st century street. Where the Burke Burnett Building meets the sidewalk with classical engaged columns, Bank One offers a hint of pilasters and a visual conversation in polychrome brick, a lesson for pedestrians in the economics of modern construction.

The Bank One Building also provides a much sought-after kind of workplace— high ceilinged, light-industrial loft spaces like those built in big American cities before and after World War I—in a new, high-performance building combining advanced electronic communications infrastructure with the rediscovered virtues of double-hung

Opposite: Facing east toward Sundance Square, Throckmorton Street elevation uses window and masonry patterns and recessed lobby to suggest a traditional entrance front. The adjoining garage, in shadow at far right, lets many tenants park on the same level as their offices.

windows. Speculative and with a modest budget, rectangular in plan and elevation, the project was expanded from eight floors to twelve during design development to accommodate offices displaced when the original bank tower next door suffered tornado damage.

The windows are a key ingredient here. Nearly eight feet tall and made by a residential manufacturer, Bank One's include single and twin units as well as "Chicago" windows, two single, operable units flanking a larger, fixed pane.

Defining a traditional base, brick and cast stone piers and entablature frame tall retail floor windows and a second floor "mezzanine." Above this, single windows occur mostly in groups of three, in stacks that add vertical emphasis, and in a continuous top floor rank that defines a giant fascia between simple cornices of brick corbels and cast stone. Interwoven with the horizontally proportioned Chicago windows, the brick street front becomes a symmetrical tartan. Aided by a subtle shift in brick color, it suggests a center bay above the entrance, flanked by twin pavilions and twin end bays. On the two lower floors colored brick forms a vivid diaper pattern at a smaller, human scale. Almost all this richness plays out in two dimensions.

With the help of computer modeling, the architects were able to study multiple alternatives for the four-color system of decoratively patterned brick cladding that spans the building, ultimately delivering construction documents that locate each individual brick.

In one more gesture to pedestrians, a wide, deeply recessed entrance shelters passersby with the help of a verdigris metal and glass canopy. The lobby inside adds more practical, user-friendly features: windows looking into adjacent retail spaces, alcoves for seats and a concierge desk, Desert Blush marble wainscoting, patterned terrazzo floors, and a straight path to the elevators.

The lobby level and many upper floors provide direct access to the parking garage that fills out the city block. Although built concurrently, offices and garage present separate visual identities: the offices a trim dark red slab, the garage a light-colored Deco-inspired structure on busy Third Street, transitioning to plain concrete on Taylor Street around the corner.

Both retail and office space feature an exposed reinforced concrete structural system that uses round, flared "mushroom" columns combined with dropped slabs. A 1905 design employed for decades in industrial lofts throughout the United States, this flared-capital construction proved economical as well as visually interesting in these high-ceilinged spaces.

Leases require that interior construction maintain the building's loft character,

Above and Right: Office building employs varied fenestration, cornices of corbelled brick and cast stone, and patterned, polychrome brick to subdivide a simple block into base, middle and top. Floor to slab height of fourteen feet and nine-foot-tall windows add generosity of scale, seen in detail at right.

keeping exposed utilities and unobstructed windows. The owners originally sought to attract dot.com companies with this slightly edgy design. It has since proved appealing to top brokerage houses and investment firms, proving the true adaptability of the loft idea and, one would like to think, a latent demand for this kind of alternative to the standard corporate workplace.

Above and Right: Projecting from the two-story recess at the main lobby, a metal and glass canopy gives pedestrians shelter and a visible entry point along the sidewalk. Detail above shows four-color patterned brickwork concentrated at the two lower floors.

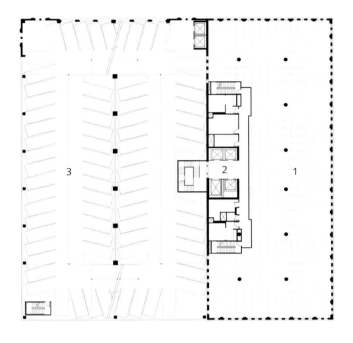

Typical Floor Plan

1. Office
2. Elevator Lobby
3. Parking Garage

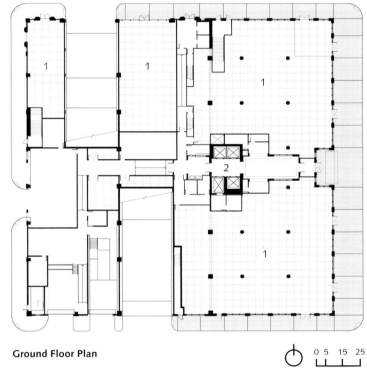

Ground Floor Plan

1. Retail Tenant Space
2. Elevator Lobby

0 5 15 25

Right: In typical tenant space, loft-style interiors, with exposed ceiling slabs and ductwork and mushroom column capitals, help maximize natural light throughout the floor. Tenant interior design here by Bob Brendle, Gensler, Dallas.

Opposite: Adjacent retail spaces, concierge desk and seating alcove enliven the entry lobby, with its Spanish and Italian marble details and a bordered terrazzo floor.

Hall Residence and Winery

RUTHERFORD, CALIFORNIA 2002

Site Plan

1. Main House
2. Garage/Caretaker
3. Guest House
4. Tennis Court

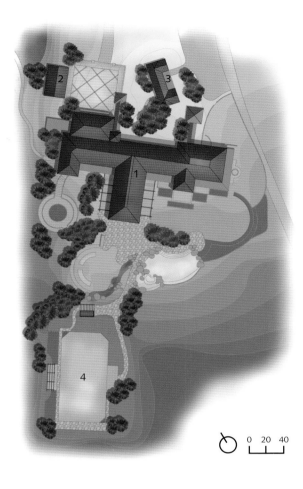

0 20 40

Rutherford Hill overlooks the Napa Valley and has had vineyards on its slopes long enough to merit its own appellation. It was a natural choice for Craig and Kathryn Hall, experienced managers and oenophiles who became full time vintners on land here and elsewhere in Napa. This vineyard is now the home of the small and highly regarded Hall Rutherford Winery, set into the hillside, and of the Halls themselves, in a house at the top of the hill.

The owners brought a taste for art collecting and entertaining, and no rigid stylistic preference, to their house project; they hoped for something simple and appropriate to the site.

A 1950-vintage ranch style house occupied the hilltop, and this provided a starting point for an essentially new structure. The architects worked with the eight-foot nine-inch plate height of the old house, using a variety of devices to add higher volumes and taller proportions, but keeping the ranch's basic horizontal line. Low copper hip roofs, stucco walls, limestone floors and terraces, and long pergolas with white-painted columns create a casual, pan-Mediterranean expression in keeping with the traditions of both viniculture and California.

Visitors arrive at a broad entrance court framed by an existing small house, a guest house, and the two-story guest wing of the main house, where a free-standing pergola and small tower mark the entrance. Inside the vestibule an interior loggia spans between the guest wing and the library and master suite, bisected at ninety degrees by the central, Great Room wing.

The Great Room design deals with the challenge of a large space and low ceiling height in two ways. It builds a tray ceiling into the volume of the hip roof, illuminated by a long skylight monitor at the roof ridge. And it steps the floors down the hill, maintaining a uniform head height for the room's many French doors by adding transoms at the lowest, living area level. A curved flight of steps and an arc of display shelves define a circular dining area at the center of the space. A few steps above this, a family sitting area includes the original fireplace, and opens to the kitchen breakfast bar and a billiard room.

The library, lined with custom Lacewood bookcases and paneling in a simple, modern design, leads to the private study and master bedroom. Here again French doors open to pergolas, terraces, and long views of vines and valley. Between the house and the vineyards, garden terraces provide space for a swimming pool and tennis court.

The winery, completed in 2005 a short distance away, is a combination of advanced technology and traditional forms and methods, dedicated to making small quantities of wine from the growth of the adjacent Sacrashe vineyard. The custom-fabricated fermentation system uses traditional gravity flow in 14,000 square feet of fermentation caves, centered on a series of groin vaults built by an Austrian craftsman using salvaged, handmade Austrian brick. The caves include a subterranean art and sculpture gallery that functions as a reception and tasting room. Directly above, a hospitality room and terrace designed by the architects treats visitors to wide views of the Napa Valley.

Opposite: From parking court, columned pergola leads to tower that marks the main entrance.

Following Pages: Seen from vineyard, the house stretches across its hilltop.

Above: Beyond terraces and pergolas, tall French doors and clerestory windows bring natural light into the Great Room beyond.

Opposite: At the private entry garden between the main house and guest house, decorative rafter tails support thin-edged integral gutters at the porch eaves.

Top: Here seen from bed alcove, guest suite sitting area opens to vineyard views.

Above: From the lowest of the three Great Room tiers, doors open to dining terrace and pool.

Opposite: The Great Room focuses on a dramatically open, intermediate-level dining area. Continuous roof monitor and tall, uniform-height doors surround the space with natural light.

Above: In the library, custom Lacewood cabinetry, doors, and paneling surround a Secession-style seating group.

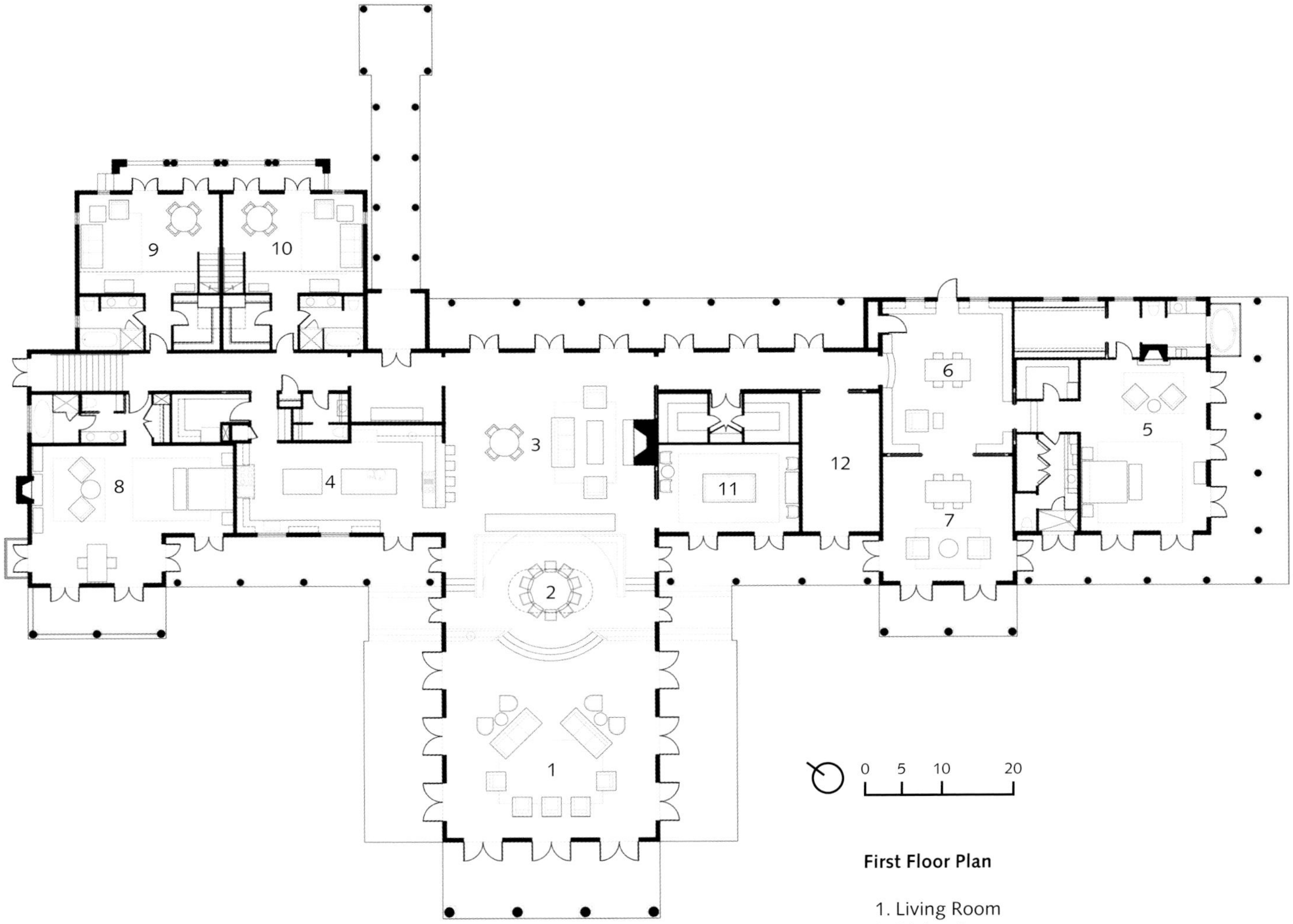

First Floor Plan

1. Living Room
2. Dining Room
3. Family Room
4. Kitchen
5. Master Bedroom
6. Library
7. Study
8. Guest Suite
9. Bedroom
10. Bedroom
11. Game Room
12. Exercise Room

Above: Master bedroom suite occupies a private, unobstructed corner with two exposures open to vineyards and mountains beyond.

Opposite: In guest suite bath, tub and frameless glass shower enjoy a window on private gardens.

Above: From main cross vault of the ageing caves,
the cave's main vault leads to a hospitality room.

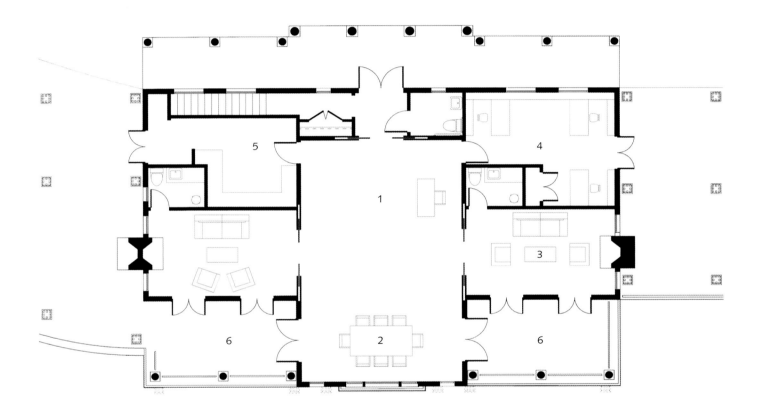

First Floor Plan

1. Hospitality Room
2. Dining/Tasting
3. Salon
4. Office
5. Catering/Kitchen
6. Terrace

Above: Above the winery caves, a hospitality room overlooks the Napa Valley.

Above: The winery's outdoor hospitality, dining and entertainment terrace commands views of the Napa Valley.

Beringer Winery

NAPA, CALIFORNIA 2002

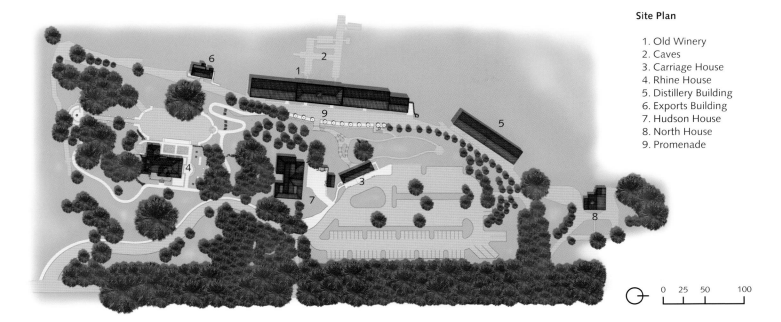

Site Plan

1. Old Winery
2. Caves
3. Carriage House
4. Rhine House
5. Distillery Building
6. Exports Building
7. Hudson House
8. North House
9. Promenade

0   25   50   100

One of America's oldest and most diversified winemakers, Beringer understands its business as partly a matter of aspirations. Attracting beginning consumers with affordable wines, it promotes reserve versions as a step up, and later, through education and experience, nurtures a desire for top-rated vintages. Visitor programs at Beringer's several California estates are a growing part of this strategy, supported in recent years by several firm projects.

The Beringer brothers' original seventeen-acre property, in the Napa Valley near St. Helena, is both a wine center and a draw in itself. Vineyards planted in the 1870's and stone winery buildings adjoin horticulturally important gardens and the 1884 Frederick Beringer family home, the iconic Rhine House. Listed on the National Register of Historic Places, this house served for years as a venue for tours, tastings, classes, sales, and special events. By the 21st century, however, visitors had overwhelmed its capacity, with maintenance needs exacerbating problems of parking, orientation, and long visitor and customer wait times.

The architects first came here to assist Beringer with a strategic master plan

Opposite: Carriage House archway frames view of restored Old Winery; blue umbrellas seen in distance shade tables along new promenade.

considering restoration, site planning and design of the property as a whole. They focused from the start on the visitor experience, analyzing conditions and opportunities with respect to historic buildings, gardens, vineyards, pedestrian and vehicle circulation, tours, and activities, plus the suitability of resources and sites for restoration and development. Owner and architects also agreed that restoration and reuse of historic structures were keys to the plan, including a cooperative relationship with the State Historic Preservation Officer, the National Park Service, and the City of St. Helena.

The plan recommended shifting most visitor functions from the Rhine House to nearby buildings such as the Old Winery and Caves, a formidable stone complex built in 1876. One of California's oldest winemaking facilities, it was being used mostly for storage, and needed repairs and seismic upgrades.

Before reuse could start, however, issues of parking, visitor services and site circulation called for attention. Phase I implementation began with a new, larger parking area further from the main gate, enabling removal of cars from the Rhine House gardens, and addressing public safety, accessibility, and site maintenance issues.

With no existing building close by, the

architects designed a new gateway structure here, the Carriage House. Its wide, barn-like arches with stone quoining reveal a wood-ceilinged concierge center, where attendants greet visitors and help them choose among tours, events, or self-guided walks. At a separate office nearby, visitors who might once have carried their wine purchases around the estate can arrange to pick them up here and have them loaded into their vehicles upon departure.

The Carriage House's open archway frames a view of the Old Winery, reachable via steps or a ramped path through a new entry garden designed with landscape architects The Olin Partnership. This project also added a tour meeting place and promenade with pollarded trees and outdoor tables at the Old Winery entrance.

Phase II, undertaken in conjunction with Architectural Resources Group, relocated many of the functions that had overburdened the Rhine House to new facilities inserted into the restored Old Winery's north wing. The long, two-story-high interior of the Old Winery's north wing now centers on an exhibit space, where visitors find public wine-tasting areas at one end, and at the other end private tasting rooms. The tasting areas and retail uses occupy freestanding, modular, one-story structures that incorporate all

added mechanical systems and utilities while leaving the original stone bearing walls and ceiling trusses intact and visible, an historic preservation benefit. New tasting bars and retail display furniture reuse redwood salvaged from the fermentation tanks that once filled the space. One of these sixteen foot high

Below: In Carriage House vestibule, departing visitors stop at pick-up counter for help collecting, loading their wine orders.

Opposite: A new entry garden leads to renovated Old Winery and Caves.

tanks, repaired and left in place, can now be viewed from the open stair that leads to a second floor function room.

The Old Winery work also included clearly differentiated steel retaining wall tiebacks and steel reinforcing of wood roof trusses to meet seismic codes. Discreet additions of roof deck insulation and skylighting improve environmental performance. Exterior restoration involved cleaning and repointing stone, inserting new code-compliant doors

behind the historic barn doors, repairing windows and woodwork, and changing details and colors to approximate the building's original appearance.

With some master plan recommendations left to implement, Beringer has nonetheless greatly enhanced its relationship with customers and community at its oldest estate, combining historic preservation, revenue-producing and development activities, education, and traditional retailing in keeping with its own

Above: Beyond a new parking area, the Carriage House gives the estate a clear gateway and orientation point.

Left: Hospitality desk in the Carriage House helps introduce visitors to tours, events.

Opposite: Carriage House at dusk reveals hospitality desk as seen from parking lot.

58

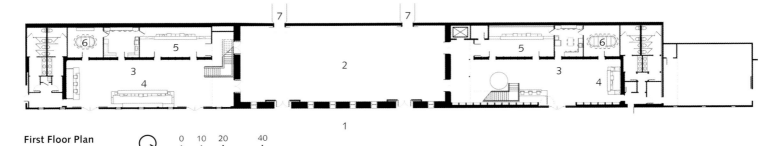

First Floor Plan

0 10 20   40

1. Promenade
2. Exhibition Space
3. Retail
4. Public Tasting
5. Tour Tasting
6. Private Tasting
7. Cave Entrance

Below: New stair in the renovated winery gives visitors a close look at a preserved, original redwood ageing tank.

Opposite: New tasting rooms and retail spaces, in freestanding structures that do not affect original construction, enliven the renovated Old Winery.

West Village

DALLAS, TEXAS 2002

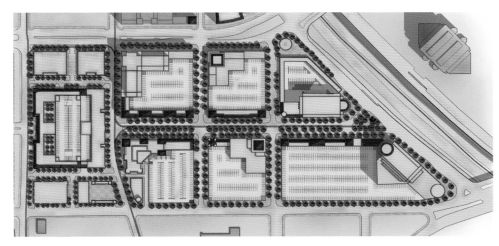

The 175 luxury apartments and over 100,000 square feet of retail space of West Village occupy a multi-block, seven-acre site near the center of Uptown, less than two miles north of the Dallas central business district.

A separately developed part of the City Place master plan, a scheme that includes larger-scale mixed-use blocks, West Village benefits from early efforts by the architects and cooperating owners to achieve pedestrian-friendly, transit-oriented urbanism in a city often characterized as car-dependent. The successful result puts a new Dallas Area Rapid Transit (DART) subway station three blocks away at the end of City Place's central street. It also establishes DART and West Village stops on the Uptown Dallas Trolley, a loop line with its own connection to downtown. Already blessed with freeway access and neat residential blocks mixed with neighborhood businesses, this part of Uptown has surfaced as a hot market for both young renters and top retailers.

Internal one-way, pedestrian-scale streets divide West Village into a 400-foot-long central block with four-story buildings wrapped around an 800-space garage, and four smaller, two-story corner blocks. Most buildings combine apartment or office uses with ground-floor retail.

Together with its structured parking, the main, central block comprises a pair of buildings, each designed as a reinforced concrete first floor retail podium

supporting three frame-and-veneer residential floors. The structures face the site's two parallel major streets—commercial McKinney Avenue on the east and residential Cole Avenue on the west—with similar apartment building programs but very different exterior styles, embodying the real estate wisdom that "like should face like."

The McKinney Avenue building evokes a downtown commercial loft in Dallas's West End, with piers and herringbone-patterned spandrels of dark brick, a grid of large double hung windows varied by wider balconies, and a hard-edged pattern of cast stone lintels, stringcourses, parapets and metal railings. The elevations subtly reveal that these are stick-built buildings on a podium, but the height, vertical proportions, and gables combine to stand up, literally and figuratively, to future City Place office buildings of ten to twenty stories. Deep alley-like "slots" articulate the long façade into a symmetrical, three-part terrace that viewers can interpret as separate structures. This symmetry adds emphasis to the central, gabled bay, a street-terminating landmark visible from the DART station.

On the Cole Avenue side, in contrast, a similar four-story building takes on a softer, almost Spanish Colonial Revival personality in keeping with neighboring apartments. Larger balconies, sloped tile roofs, and planar synthetic stucco walls suggest individual, "punched" windows in a vintage apartment hotel, an image completed by the symmetrical front

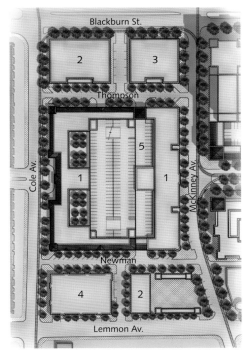

Site Plan

1. Four-Story/Residential Above Retail
2. Two-Story/Residential Above Retail
3. Two-Story/Commercial
4. Cinema Above Retail
5. Parking Garage

Opposite: Round bay announces a major West Village retail corner at intersection with McKinney Avenue.

elevation and a setback that accommodates a vehicle pull-off.

The high-ceilinged first floor spaces of these buildings readily accommodate generous, upscale retail uses. The parking structure that fills much of the block's interior also benefits from this first floor height; landscaped setbacks and a walkable alley here make an attractive urban space.

The north and south sides of the central block front on the four lower, smaller blocks, designed to enforce slow moving vehicular traffic and encourage street life. The meticulously detailed two-story buildings here exhibit a range of vernacular personalities from the 1910's through the 1940's, using generous windows, brick, synthetic stucco, and cast stone.

The exceptional structure here is the Magnolia Theater, a popular art-movie venue that occupies a whole block, with the theater above and street level retail and restaurants below. The resulting blank upper façades display rows of striated stucco piers and shallow, tall niches filled with geometric-patterned colored ceramic tiles in lieu of windows. These continue the street rhythm of small commercial bays, building up to the movie-palace glamour of the Texas Deco entrance tower, complete with silver marquee, neon-lighted pylons, and sleek escalator to the main lobby.

West Village presents an interesting comparison to Frisco Town Square: both developments are centered on four-story,

mixed-use buildings, with a detailed and sensitive response to context at West Village, and the need to create a context from almost nothing, at Frisco. The instant availability of public transportation and high-quality retail at West Village creates a dramatic, but perhaps temporary lifestyle advantage. In both cases, however, the architects have provided a clear statement about how an urban building should meet the street, what the pedestrian experience should be like, and how to integrate parking—all issues worth noting throughout this book.

Above: Arched parking garage entrance (center of photo) is easily seen yet integrated with adjacent shop fronts.

Opposite: Beyond parapet, a second floor roof terrace provides outdoor space for loft apartments. Flanking wings balance the building's horizontal lines and create a more varied streetscape

64

Left: Residential entrance along Cole Avenue is set back to accommodate an auto drop-off. Southwestern style details respond to the stucco and red tile palette of neighboring apartment buildings.

Below Left: Cast stone band courses and pilaster caps, polychrome brick lend two-story commercial building a distinctive identity.

Opposite: On the central McKinney Avenue building, ironspot bricks in herringbone pattern animate spandrels and balconies. Visual references to Dallas's early 20th century loft-commercial buildings anticipate large-scale office structures planned for opposite side of street.

Below: Marking Magnolia Theater entrance, neon traces the corner tower's Texas Deco details.

Below Right Top: Cinema's corner tower announces street level lobby and ticketing area; escalators take patrons to second floor main lobby.

Below Right Bottom: Pilasters flanking arched parapets modulate the block-long Magnolia Theater elevation. Cinema occupies second floor above street level shops and restaurants.

Opposite: Window-like niches, ornamented with water-jet cut ceramic tile patterns, punctuate the cinema façade (detail at left).

Cook Children's Medical Center North Pavilion

FORT WORTH, TEXAS 2003

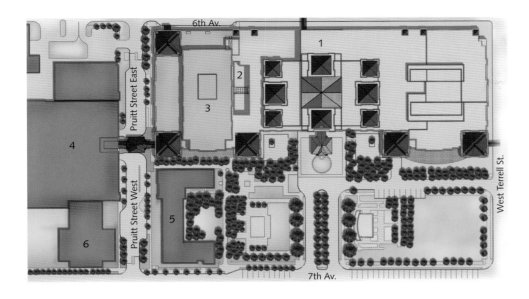

Site Plan

1. Existing Main Hospital
2. Courtyard
3. New Hospital Inpatient
   Expansion
4. North Garage
5. Administration Building
6. Easter Seals Building

0   50   100   200

Begun in 1985 and expanded by the architects eight times since, the Cook Children's Medical Center originated in the merger of two established hospitals, concerned from the beginning that their new, larger building, at a location distinctive only for a new freeway interchange, should have a clear architectural identity. The original trustees strongly supported the idea of a building that would speak directly to parents and children through evident warmth and careful, family-friendly design.

The five-story North Pavilion is the latest and largest of the eight expansion projects to date, providing space for eighty new beds. The first two floors include a new cardiac care unit, a new pediatric intensive care unit with its own waiting area and adjacent landscaped courtyard, and doubled capacity for the original neonatal intensive care unit. Intensive care nursing units, on the second floor, integrate two-room bedside nurse stations and conventional nurse stations to ease information exchange among professionals and other staff members. On the ground floor is a new auditorium and conference center, used for medical rounds and in-house training as well as other professional and public programs.

In exterior massing the North Pavilion takes the form of a subordinate tower connected to the main tower by a two-story hyphen. It steps down again to a comfortable two stories along pedestrian-friendly Pruitt Street, where the taller masses disappear from view. The North Pavilion has its own public entrance a few steps from the parking garage across the street.

Consistent with the original building, the design is based on a conceptual kit of parts, with alternating bays of grouped and single windows on twelve-foot modules, employing custom color glazed brick, Texas limestone, and occasional blue, pyramidal metal roofs. The entrance pylons and glazed canopy, which make explicit the origins of the Center's architecture in Texas Deco and the work of Paul Cret, repeat an earlier design used at the main entrance and covered walkways.

The architects produced alternate three, four, and five story tower designs for the Center's consideration, a typical practice for the firm. The choice of five stories trades higher first cost for life-cycle economy and flexibility. As built, the topmost floors include unfinished shell space for future expansion.

Past the sidewalk pylons, the entrance brings users onto a wide, clear-span bridge, the upper level of a two-story volume roughly forty-eight feet square,

Left: Seen from pedestrian Pruitt Street, upper floors of North Pavilion recede from view, reinforcing a comfortable, two-story scale.

Opposite: View from parking structure shows full height of North Pavilion expansion.

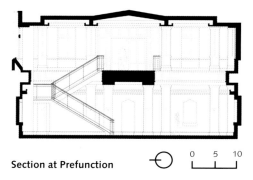

Section at Prefunction 0 5 10

70

with generous natural light and an indirectly lighted coffered ceiling. The bridge with its polished granite floor pattern and tic-tac-toe design glazed railing feeds directly into the Center's system of public corridors. To one side, a two-flight stair leads to the ground floor space below, which functions as a public lounge, a lobby for the auditorium, and a prefunction space for the conference center. The simplified order of pilasters and ceiling coffers in this space continues in the auditorium, where wall panels and paired, engaged half-columns enhance acoustic performance.

On the patient floors as throughout the hospital, repeated color variations and decorative elements serve the need for orientation and a sense of continuity. To provide an engaging environment for sick children, the design also adds elements of architectural surprise and humor, always with a respectful, light touch. Nurse stations have their own colored "pylons," for example, and patterns in tile floors and glass block walls depict kids at play.

The Cook Children's Medical Center has received wide recognition as a model of its kind. Like the Tarrant County Family Law Center, although with a vastly more complex program, this hospital center effectively balances the need for a sense of context and architectural dignity appropriate to its purpose, and the need on the part of stressed, anxious families for a supportive environment, a "clean well-lighted place."

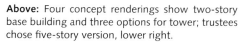

Above: Four concept renderings show two-story base building and three options for tower; trustees chose five-story version, lower right.

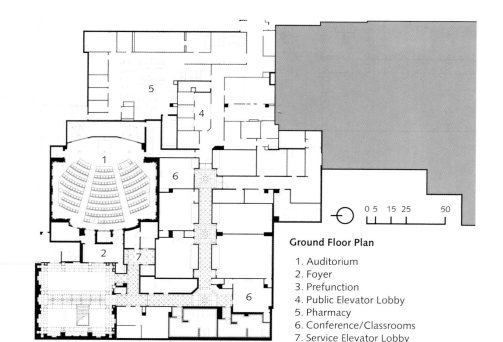

Ground Floor Plan

1. Auditorium
2. Foyer
3. Prefunction
4. Public Elevator Lobby
5. Pharmacy
6. Conference/Classrooms
7. Service Elevator Lobby

0 5 15 25 50

Top: From Pruitt Street entrance, bridge crosses double height pre-function lobby to main corridor; railing's glass panels display signature tic-tac-toe motif.

Above: Auditorium illustrates system of coved ceilings, direct and indirect lighting, wall panels and paired pilasters seen throughout the building.

Left: Pre-function space serves auditorium, with direct access to entrance bridge above.

Hawken School Natatorium

GATES MILLS, OHIO   2003

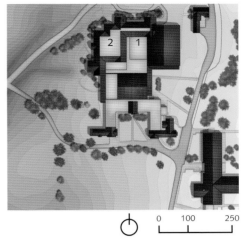

Site Plan

1. New Athletic Center Lobby
2. New Pool

0   100   250

The firm's role in restoring and expanding Severance Hall, the home of the Cleveland Orchestra, not only provided an introduction to the Hawken School, but also opened a small window on the history of its upper school campus in Gates Mills, Ohio. In the years before World War I, Severance's architects, Frank Walker and Harry Weeks, joined the international fox hunting and polo playing set that gathered in Gates Mills, generously supported by White Motor Company co-founder Windsor White. The White family country house designed by Walker & Weeks survives as the Hawken campus's oldest building. The Chagrin Valley Hunt still rides, but few traces remain of White's extensive horse farm on this site.

Hawken School is a pre-K through twelve independent school with two campuses in the Greater Cleveland area—a lower/middle school campus in Lyndhurst and the upper school campus in Gates Mills. Originally small schools on historic properties, both expanded with little in the way of a facility program or master plan.

The architects became involved in an effort to create ten-year master plans for each campus, setting short-and long-term facility goals, and establishing an architectural character for the Hawken School as a whole. The agenda includes existing condition assessments, infrastructure and circulation studies, landscape, site and building concept plans, and implementation strategies. Although planning is still underway, school and architects have agreed to treat each campus as an academic village, with appropriate forms such as town greens and main streets. Beyond this, the school has embraced "visual literacy," adding a basic grounding in architecture and environmental design to its institutional goals.

Meanwhile, a new upper school natatorium emerged as a building priority, for two reasons. First, there was a need to rework the entrance drive and improve the visitor's initial view of mismatched gymnasium buildings and covered walks students called "porches to nowhere." A major athletic center upgrade would bring with it the opportunity to control and improve this view. Second, competitive swimming is a Hawken phenomenon, with a program that claims world-record holders, Olympians, and a dominant percentage of state titles. A new natatorium would focus attention, and contributions, on a new Hawken image.

The resulting project evokes the stables that once occupied this site. Barn-like gable ends with tall arches, used for both light and ventilation, establish rhythm and height in keeping with the tall spaces inside. Two contiguous new elevations wrap the corner of the existing athletic complex, reshaping the view from the entrance road. The elevation facing entering traffic centers on a tall arched window that marks the long axis of the new eight-lane, 25-yard competition pool. Setback gable ends turn the corner to the symmetrical front elevation. Here a low porch fronts the new common lobby shared by the new pool and the remodeled varsity field house, formerly the intramural gym.

Below: New building complements a picturesque view from campus main entrance.

Opposite: Seen from entrance drive, natatorium visually breaks mass of athletic center beyond.

The two major new interiors, the common lobby and the competition pool space, employ high-vaulted spaces framed with dark, exposed steel roof trusses that suggest the structure of a traditional barn roof or, less literally, a neo-medieval academic hall. New ancillary spaces include the pool's spectator seating, locker rooms, and support facilities, for a total of some 30,000 square feet of new construction.

In addition to the nearby White House, for their detailing the architects looked closely at the prosperous fin-de-siecle farms of the Chagrin and Cuyahoga valleys. These mixed the 1830's Greek Revival of Ohio's Connecticut Western Reserve with the Shingle Style, all rendered here in narrow, white-painted lap siding as well as shingles.

The donation of a fine weathervane in the form of a hawk—the school symbol and mascot, naturally enough—for the cupola over the main entrance suggests that the school community has indeed embraced the natatorium as a step toward a new image, one rooted in an old image still well remembered in history-conscious Gates Mills.

Right: Cupola weathervane marks athletic center as home of The Hawks.

Opposite: Stepped gable ends break down scale of natatorium addition, recall style of White family stables that once occupied site.

Following Pages: The massing of the main entry responds to human scale, creating the feel of a porch and paddock area in contrast to the adjacent large gables. Details pay homage to the 19th century Western Reserve style of Northeastern Ohio.

First Floor Plan

1. Pool
2. Field House (Reconfigured Gym)
3. Courtyard
4. Weight Room
5. Wrestling Room
6. Old Gym
7. New Campus Entry
8. Shared Lobby

Opposite and Below: A new common lobby serves the natatorium, field house, and other athletic center facilities beyond. Image below highlights the trim and wainscot which reflect the details of a tack room and address the agrarian history of the property.

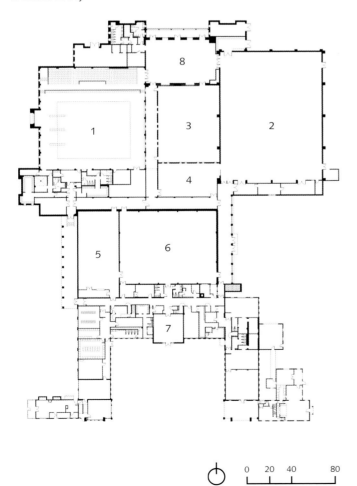

0   20   40   80

80

Left: Flanked by photos, interior windows along main athletic center corridor view pool, reinforce school pride in Hawken's champion swimmers.

Opposite: Bleacher seating, barn-inspired steel trusses lend sense of scale to vast competition pool.

82

Above: The duct work is woven into the trusses to create a more pleasing aesthetic.

Opposite: On long side of pool, bay window and gable frame diving board.

Dr Pepper Ballpark

FRISCO, TEXAS 2003

Minor League baseball has enjoyed renewed popularity across the country, rediscovered by American families seeking the kind of relaxing, affordable afternoon pastime that professional sports now rarely offers. At Dr Pepper Ballpark the priority is the park, a green enclosure where kids can play and families can picnic, meet their neighbors, and watch warm-ups in the bullpen.

The architects' response here is an appropriately different way to watch baseball. It trades the usual steel grandstand for a cost-saving combination of earth-moving and lightweight pavilions that revisit valued American ideas about recreational design.

The emphasis on community extends beyond game day. Contemporary stadiums and civic sports facilities typically serve as economic catalysts and, sometimes, physical anchors for local real estate development, ideas these architects have worked with since their competition-winning proposal for the Texas Rangers' complex, The Ballpark at Arlington. The master plan for Dr Pepper Ballpark, on sixty-five acres of prairie twenty miles north of Dallas, is smaller but goes a step further. It envisions this Double-A league field as not only an investment catalyst, but the physical and social center of a neighborhood that will mix multi-family residential, hotel, office, retail, restaurant and entertainment uses. Streets and a public plaza are already in place, awaiting mid-rise buildings that will overlook the landscaped ballpark and conceal structured and surface parking at the rear.

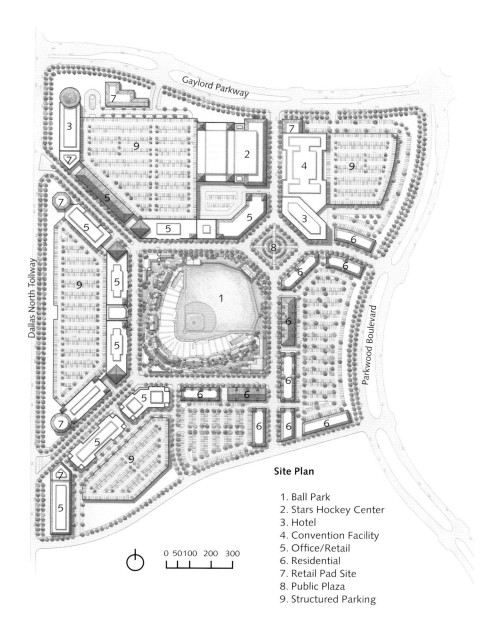

Site Plan

1. Ball Park
2. Stars Hockey Center
3. Hotel
4. Convention Facility
5. Office/Retail
6. Residential
7. Retail Pad Site
8. Public Plaza
9. Structured Parking

85

As a first step in implementing the plan, the client team of public and private entities needed to build a stadium within a twenty-four-month schedule and roughly $25 million budget.

Picturing a ballpark that would double as a landscaped town park, the architects warmed to the idea of earth-supported seating. This was achieved by lowering the whole playing field fourteen feet, using a design strategy pioneered by the 1913 Yale Bowl. Placing most seats below existing grade enabled building the remaining superstructure—twenty-nine luxury suites, restaurant, concession stands, restrooms, press box, and support facilities—on grade at the lip of the bowl, in the form of separate, economical stick-built pavilions of two to four levels.

The architects looked closely at the coastal vernacular of Galveston, Texas to give these structures an image that is both evocative and appropriate. In general they employ the chamfered posts and light steel roof trusses of old-fashioned grandstands, somewhat streamlined and rationalized. Behind home plate, where the viewing structures rise to four stories and a group of enclosed elevator and stair towers, box offices and radio station facilities cluster to provide a windbreak, the architectural expression adds a touch of Coney Island castle, with an asymmetrical roofscape of belvederes and cupolas and a lighted sign to mark this main entrance gate

Opposite: The home plate building visually encloses the seating bowl; in the foreground, the visitor's bullpen is located within the seating bowl.

on the prairie. Materials are tough and sustainable, especially metal standing seam roofs, metal roof trusses, and cementitious siding.

Moving earth rather than erecting structural steel, and phasing the bowl and the stick-built structures independently rather than assembling a monolithic stadium, saved construction money and time. An additional, continuing payoff lies in the reduced operating and maintenance cost of the on-grade, street level concourses, which deliver clear circulation with relatively few stairs, ramps, or elevators.

These savings helped pay for the elegant perimeter fence with its steel bat-and-ball grille. Recalling a gated, private London square and serving somewhat the same function, it protects the landscaped concourse and adds value to the prime building sites across the street, ready for the next development phase of this innovative baseball village.

Left: From site's southwest corner, main entrance walkway leads straight to home plate pavilion, with glimpse of green ballfield beyond.

Above: Corner buildings house team office and box offices; at right of photo, mid-block fences open views of park and batting cage.

Left: Entered from the green concourse/park, pavilions contain restrooms and concessions at ground level and suites above.

Opposite: Seen here from a suite balcony, on-grade concourse below provides circulation while doubling as an urban park.

90

This Page: Pavilions contain services and concessions at concourse level; upper level spaces include the club lounge (top left) and suites with open balconies (center left) and enclosed spaces (left) accommodating fourteen people.

Opposite Left: After dark the ballpark's many lighted towers enliven the skyline and create points of reference for patrons.

Opposite Top Right: Open-air bridges connect all levels of the pavilions.

Opposite Bottom Right: Details throughout reflect baseball symbols and traditions and the civic character of the park.

92 **Main Concourse Plan**

1. Main Entry
2. Outfield Entry
3. Entry Courtyard
4. Garden Concourse
5. Inner Concourse
6. Outfield Concourse
7. General Seating
8. Berm Seating
9. Concession
10. Restroom
11. Team Store
12. Ticketing
13. Team Admin./Maint.
14. Loading/Commissary
15. Bullpen
16. Batting Cage

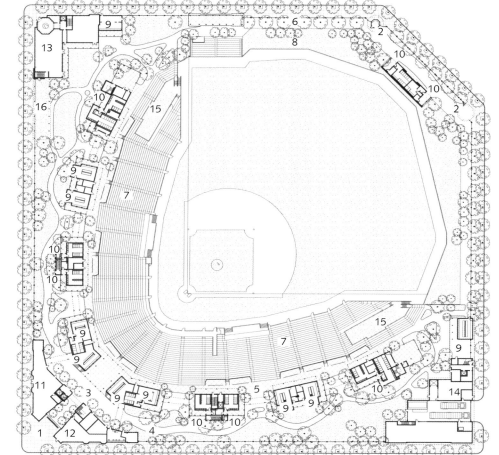

Upper Level Plan

1. Suites
2. Club Restaurant
3. Covered Porch
4. Kitchen
5. Restroom
6. Meeting Facility
7. Team Offices

Section at Home Plate

1. Main Entry
2. Garden Concourse
3. Concession
4. Inner Concourse
5. Club Restaurant
6. Suite
7. Press Box

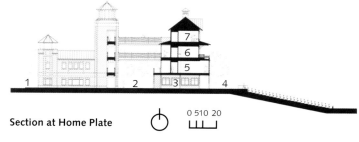

Opposite: The home plate building houses concession, suites, and a press box while blocking the prevailing southwest winds.

Frisco Square

FRISCO, TEXAS 2004

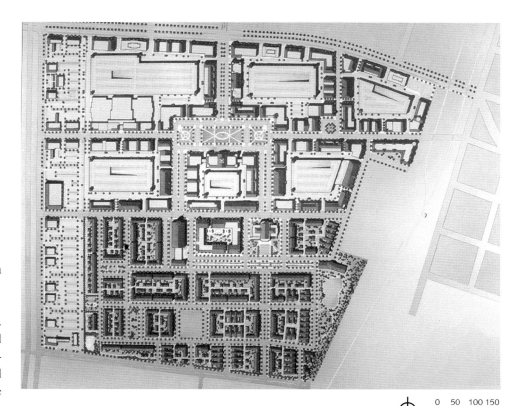

Master Plan

0   50   100 150

Frisco Square is a work in progress on a truly urban scale.

The city of Frisco, Texas has big plans. Named for the railroad that provided its initial reason for being, later a bedroom community, and recently rated the fastest-growing jurisdiction in the Dallas-Fort Worth metroplex, Frisco could become home to 250,000 people within twenty years. The architects' master plan for Frisco Square is similarly aspirational.

As projected, this privately-developed city center covers some 140 acres and two main districts: a mixed-use commercial area fronting on arterial roads and focused on a city hall square, and a mostly residential enclave of row houses and small parks. A parcel of land owned by the city was incorporated into the master plan and distributed throughout the project as sites for parks, open spaces and civic buildings.

Buildings along the arterial frontage roads will invite motorists, but will form a relatively continuous wall with most parking at the rear. Blocks near the central square will have a more urban character, similar to the four-story mixed-use block wrapped around structured parking at Dallas's West Village. Four-story limestone-faced buildings and a continuous, neoclassical arcade will surround the square itself—more like the arcaded streets of Turin than the Latin American-style market plaza at Grand Avenue in Southlake.

Beyond the square, the row house neighborhood will follow English Regency precedents, with symmetrical terraces of brick houses, small rear yards, and an alley or mews for parking and ancillary buildings. Nearly half of these houses will front on a park, square, or landscaped boulevard.

Based on this master plan, and a planning and design code written by the the firm's team, several architectural firms have been involved in creating the first buildings of Frisco Town Square, including the city hall and residential blocks. Additional architects recruited to design row houses include Albert, Righter & Tittmann, Centerbrook Architects, Demetri Porphyrios, and Robert A. M. Stern.

The firm's buildings illustrated here define the first four-story block of Coleman Street, the main gateway from the highway to the city hall square. This early construction priority includes some of the limestone-faced, arcaded buildings facing the main square, so that this one street provides a prototype for Frisco Square's mixed-use core.

The first floors of these buildings provide high-ceilinged, flexible commercial space that can accommodate a grand lobby or a retail or restaurant interior with a balcony. In general, the upper floors of the buildings at the ends of blocks are designed for office space, while the brick-faced mid-block buildings contain apartments. Each long residential building façade is visually divided, as at West Village, by "slots" that suggest a symmetrical group of three buildings. In addition, each façade incorporates deeply-recessed balconies with cast stone balustrades. At least one apartment building enriches these openings with neoclassical arches and pilasters at the second and third floors, matching the two-story order of pilasters that appears on the main square. Although these neo-Renaissance details have local precedents—for example, Dallas's 1902 Wilson Building—the unified, neo-Renaissance streetscape planned here is

Opposite: Mixed-use buildings line Coleman Avenue, the main boulevard leading from the highway to the town square. Articulations and recessed balconies break up the brick street front of this retail/residential building

96

rare in America. (One comparable design is the four-story housing prototype for New York City designed by McKim, Mead and White in 1903, the King Model Houses, but that is purely residential.)

As seen elsewhere in this book, the critical question is what will happen where the buildings meet the street. Frisco Square has the physical potential to create a European-style street life of charm and energy. Its social and economic climate is still being defined, however, and

the owners and architects must hope that this place will grow beyond neighborhood amenity status to become the citywide and regional attraction it aspires to be.

Above and Opposite: Arched, two-story openings, with recessed balconies and cast stone balustrades, clearly mark the center of a block (see overall view above) and emphasize this residential building's main entrance among flanking shopfronts.

Above: Visible at left and right of photo, deep recesses maintain Frisco Street residential building's continuity while suggesting a freestanding structure.

Opposite: Closer view of residential building suggests Frisco Street's future character as an urban boulevard with mature street trees, lively storefronts and overhanging balconies.

Following Pages: Frisco Street residential block is articulated as a symmetrical composition with façade breaks, recessed and projecting balconies.

Opposite: Corner tower of office building marks intersection of Frisco Street with main square, and begins a continuous arcade designed to border the square.

Left: Texas Leuters limestone sheathes primary façades of office buildings lining the square. Custom-designed capitals and denticular cornice create pronounced shadows in the Texas sun, emphasizing façade setback at fourth floor.

104

Right: Limestone pilasters, arched window surrounds and entablature elements create an appropriate base for the office building and an elegant retail setting along the street.

Opposite: Master plan envisions extensions of this streetside arcade lining all four sides of town square.

Firewheel Town Center

GARLAND, TEXAS   2005

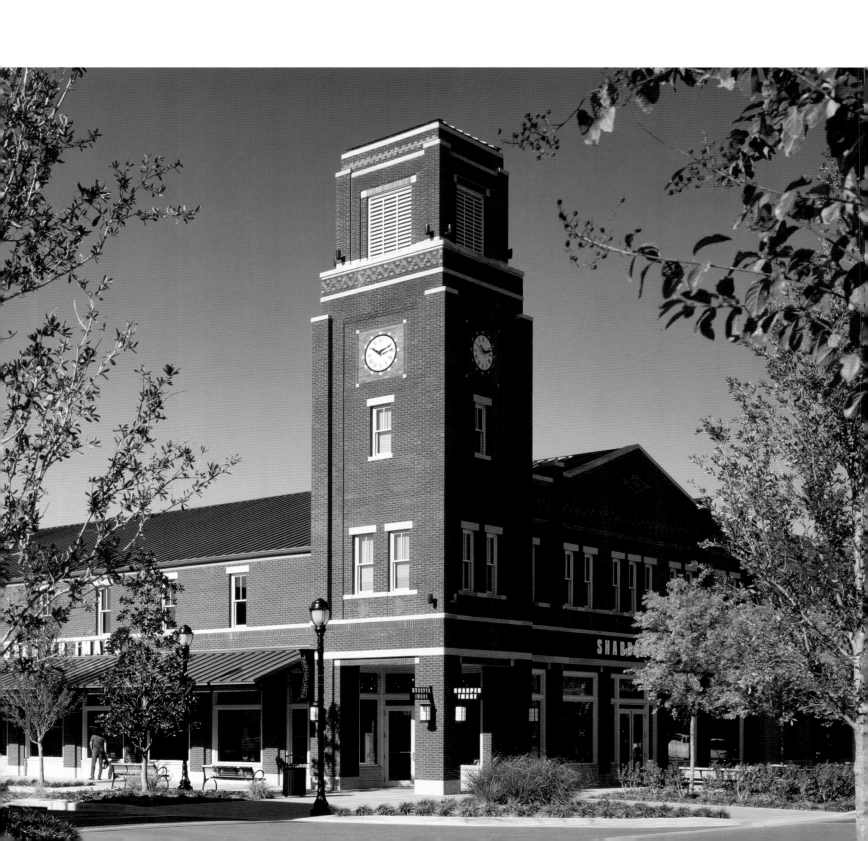

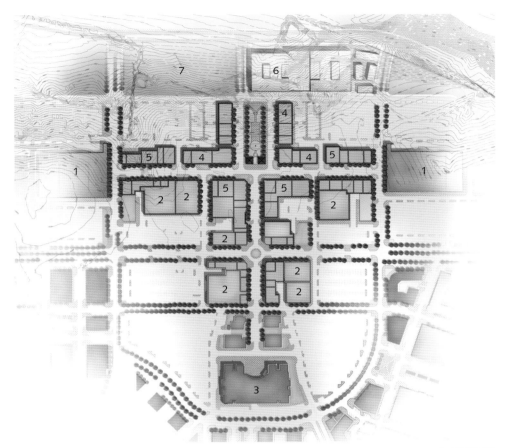

Site Plan

1. Department Store
2. Junior Anchor
3. Cinema
4. Office Above Retail
5. Retail
6. Residential
7. Future Phase

0 100 200 300

At first glance, Firewheel Town Center looks as if an entire regional mall, including anchor stores and mid-size "junior anchor" chain stores, had been asked to step outside and invited to regroup in a small, pre-1950 Texas downtown.

As for the reality: Firewheel represents a serious dialogue between a 250-year tradition of American town planning and a fifty-year body of expertise in shopping center economics and design. It is clearly part of a national trend toward so-called "open air," Main Street-like centers, which the firm explored earlier at Southlake Town Square. As at Southlake, however, the push and pull of the two traditions, Main Street and mall, begins to produce a richer, more flexible third way. There is a rational integration of cars and parking with pedestrians; a choice of walk-up and drive-up entrances to many stores; and an office component blended in—over ten percent of the total 775,000 square feet. Most important, the architects and developers subordinate these and other organizational ideas to the goal of placemaking, relearning the language of Main Street to create a pedestrian experience on the suburban prairie.

Some of the vocabulary comes from the historic main street of Garland, Texas, founded when railroads converged here in the 1880's. Highways now make this location a crossroads of the Dallas-Fort Worth suburban metroplex, midway between regional malls in Plano and Mesquite, and at the center of suburban development around Richardson, Sachse, and Rowlett northeast of Dallas.

Firewheel's plan begins with two retail-lined cross streets, Market Street and Center Street. Firewheel Drive parallels Market, bringing highway traffic to the Center Street fountain circle and parking, including lots that provide direct access to anchors such as Dillard's, and junior anchors such as Linens & Things and Barnes & Noble. A public square north of Center and Market provides a second orientation point, punctuated by the red brick "market house" clock tower and lined with two-story buildings incorporating upper level office space.

By the firm's rule of thumb, buildings on two sides of a block can be served by surface parking on the block interior, while buildings that enclose a block require structured parking in the middle. For now, surface parking lots suffice at Firewheel, supplemented by on-street parking.

Compared with Southlake, the building budget was tight here, and having larger, national chain stores called for

creative design to maintain variety and interest. In addition to colored and patterned brick, synthetic stucco was used to save money and re-create building types once typically executed in limestone. Examples include the long bank-like block with its Beaux-Arts classical pilasters and modillion cornice facing the public square, and an Art Deco-inspired façade with mill finish aluminum trim and multi-color frieze. Other creative yet economical ornament includes Viennese Secession-inspired stencil decorations including a firewheel flower, and a bas-relief roundel adapted from a standard ceiling medallion.

Custom designs for national, junior anchor retailers include a Streamline Moderne building with large show windows for a home furnishings retailer, and a neon-accented Deco "theater" block for a major electronics store.

Opposite: Clock tower of "market building" provides focal point for Firewheel Town Center.

108 Individually specified awnings, canopies, lighting fixtures and other metal details provide economical and practical variations that complement storefronts and office entrances. The streetscape design, with landscape architects SWA, adds another level of interest with street trees, traditional light posts, and an extensive program of street furniture.

While Firewheel Town Center does not yet incorporate civic facilities and is just beginning to acquire a residential component, the master plan anticipates this kind of expansion in addition to more commercial uses, with the possibility that town and town center may someday become a complete urban core.

Left: Octagonal tower adds a corner landmark, raising a commercial building to civic scale.

Opposite Top: Seen from park, synthetic stucco detail of retail block suggests an early 20th century limestone bank, typical of more traditional architectural language concentrated near the center of the project.

Opposite Bottom: Fountain, pergolas enrich a compact public park.

Following Pages: Elements of a traditional Texas main street here include alternating colors and stylistic elements, tall storefront windows, diagonal on-street parking, street lights.

112

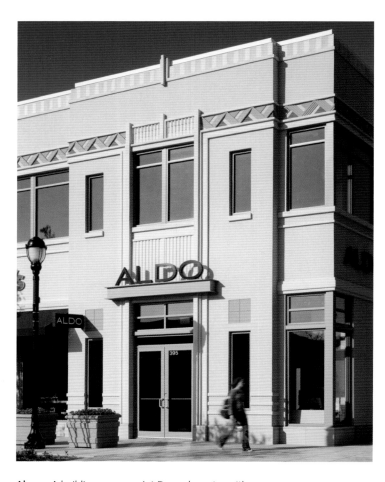

Above: A building assumes Art Deco character with corner windows, zigzag ornament.

Above Right: Several one-off designs were created for big-box tenants. Here ample amounts of glass create a greater than normal degree of transparency, while maintaining the scale of a traditional retail streetscape.

Right: Retail signage and awnings together with architectural details create a human scaled environment along the street.

Opposite: A metal and glass curtain wall spanning between brick party walls forms one of Firewheel's more contemporary buildings.

114

Above: A taut brick façade employs simple cast stone and polychrome brick details.

Right: Close-up of cast stone and polychrome brick details. Inset reveals of darker brick add vertical punctuation to an otherwise horizontal elevation.

Opposite: In a play on its home theater offerings, an electronics retailer plus several "liner" shops occupy a building designed to recall an Art Moderne cinema.

DAY SPA / SALON

Day Spa/Salon

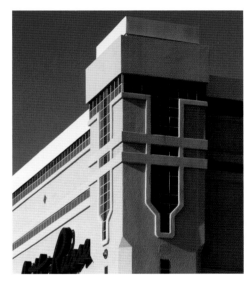

Above: Painted stencil detail on stucco wall surface is based on an abstraction of the firewheel, the wild flower that gives the project its name.

Above Top: Ceramic tile applied flush with surface of stucco sets off banded ornament at a corner pier.

Right: Synthetic stucco details and ceramic tile accents articulate this end bay of an office and retail building overlooking the central square.

Opposite: Stucco details here create stylized pilaster capitals and spandrels, and articulate the building's stepped parapet.

Tarrant County Family
Law Center

FORT WORTH, TEXAS 2005

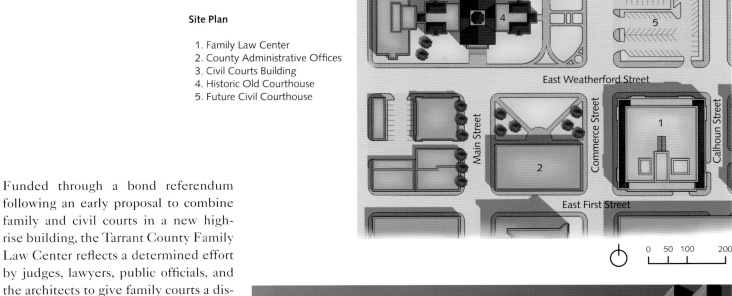

119

Site Plan

1. Family Law Center
2. County Administrative Offices
3. Civil Courts Building
4. Historic Old Courthouse
5. Future Civil Courthouse

Funded through a bond referendum following an early proposal to combine family and civil courts in a new highrise building, the Tarrant County Family Law Center reflects a determined effort by judges, lawyers, public officials, and the architects to give family courts a distinct, purpose-built home.

In addition to sharing the complex requirements that judges, marshals, and staff impose on any modern courthouse, family courts serve many new users of the justice system, coping with experiences that can be especially stressful, disorienting, or intimidating. More than most, this building-type calls for an architecture of clarity and dignity, from well-lighted courtrooms to an accessible place to park.

Urban context was as important as interior planning in establishing a sense of place. The 1895 Tarrant County Courthouse, at the end of Main Street near the site of the original Fort Worth, establishes the main point of reference opposite the site. The master plan for this area envisions another new courthouse on the vacant block to the north, grouping several new and existing buildings in a justice campus. To the south, the heterogeneous, pedestrian-oriented

Right: View shows east façade with City Center Towers in background. Projecting bays lend symmetrical order to long elevation. Window heights and details follow traditional vertical hierarchy.

Opposite: Family Law Center main entrance (lower left of photo) faces Weatherford Street. At right, High Victorian Gothic mass of Horse Fountain anchors old courthouse square.

120 Downtown Redevelopment Core presents a larger, commercial scale.

A block-filling, five-story structure, the Family Law Center is a modern building that relies on familiar conventions of Beaux Arts design—high one-story base, three-story "shaft" defining a giant order, cornice and one-story attic. Projecting corner bays correspond to the actual locations of main courtrooms. Individual three-story pilasters appear here and above the main entrance; elsewhere, window placement and size are enough to suggest a columnar wall system of classical proportions. All of this conveys civic purpose without overwhelming visitors or competing with the 1895 courthouse.

The new building shows an explicit affinity with the old courthouse where it meets the sidewalk, employing the same rusticated, Texas pink granite for its one-story base. The deep, sheltering front entrance in this granite wall balances images of authority and warmth, security and accessibility.

The upper floors in deep red brick incorporate more granite detail. Incised and studded entablatures match the old courthouse's cornice height. Stylized triglyph capitals, mullions, and carved spandrels across the exterior display the same granite in a combination of polished, thermal, and rock face finishes, paralleling some of the 1895 building's cliff-like toughness.

Public interiors are high-ceilinged and generously lighted, in a simplified but

carefully proportioned "Deco" neoclassical style. Decorations include economical custom details such as mill finish reveals on the black anodized aluminum balcony railings, feature strips set into the terrazzo floors, and a wallpaper frieze integrated with the air-handling grilles. Richer details—a gray granite wainscot, mahogany doors and surrounds—are used sparingly throughout, most often in courtrooms.

The main lobby entered directly at street level takes the form of a two-story columned atrium. Elevators and a double stair opposite the security checkpoint give access to high-traffic second-floor offices, such as those dealing with child support. Other services on lower floors include Title IV-D courtrooms and associated judicial chambers, domestic relations and family courts services, and the district attorney protective order and mental health unit.

Arranged around a second, skylit atrium and open stair, a series of courtroom suites or "sets" occupies the two top floors. Each set consists of an elected judge's district courtroom, an associate courtroom (for an appointed judge), and related judges' chambers and administrative offices. To allow for secure perimeter circulation, the design places

Right: Rusticated stonework reflects historic Tarrant County Courthouse's use of Texas Sunset Red granite in polished, thermal, and rock face finishes.

Opposite: Entrance elevation displays base, shaft, and capital organization. Recessed loggia shelters groups queuing for entry.

the associate courtrooms on the interior. The district courtrooms, which are likely to have longer trials, occupy the building corners and receive direct natural light.

Away from public view are security offices with prisoner holding facilities and sallyport, secure parking for judges and staff, and facility management offices and loading docks. An important addition to the visitor experience for the entire court system, a new, seven-level parking structure occupies the adjacent block.

Security here goes beyond the concept of physical separation or surveillance to embrace the psychological dimension of a safe, ordered, comfortable place for families. The lobby, atrium, and other spaces employ natural light, occasional access to outdoor views, and attention to small-scale detail to help create a warm, family-friendly environment.

122

Left: Family Law Center parapet matches lower parapet height of Tarrant County Courthouse, beyond at right.

Opposite: Seen in detail of bay, stylized entablature, pilaster capital, and window mullions employ same granite finishes—polished, thermal, and rock face—used at building's base. Spandrel frames a sandblasted "scales of justice" detail.

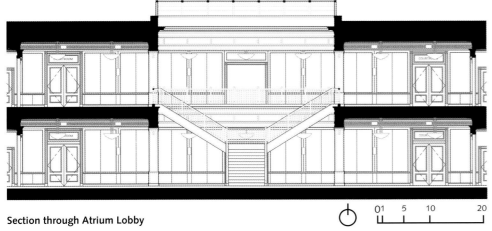

Section through Atrium Lobby

01　5　10　20

Below Left: Courtroom lobby at fourth floor opens to skylit stairwell and similar fifth floor lobby.

Below Right: Main lobby stairway leads to public functions on second floor. Lobby column capitals reflect design of building's exterior granite capitals.

Opposite: Natural light floods atrium stairwell between fourth and fifth floors (see section at left).

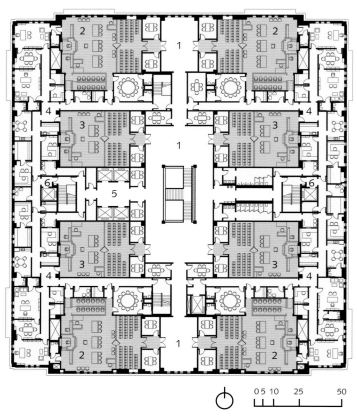

126

Fifth Floor Plan

1. Public Lobby
2. District Courtroom
3. Associate Courtroom
4. Judicial Suite
5. Public Elevators
6. Secure Elevator

0 5 10   25   50

Below: View from atrium lobby toward District Court lobby shows typical public space finishes: terrazzo floors, granite wainscoting, acoustically treated wall panels, and wallpaper frieze.

Opposite: One of eight Associate Courtrooms on fourth and fifth floors, as seen from public lobby.

Above: Placement of jury box niche to the side of litigant well reflects relatively small number of jury proceedings.

Opposite: All eight of the Family Law Center's District Courtrooms have windows, a key priority, given the long and often stressful proceedings handled in District Court.

Grand Avenue

SOUTHLAKE, TEXAS   2006

Site Plan

1. Office Above Retail & Restaurant
2. Retail & Restaurant
3. Residential
4. City Hall/Library
5. Cinema
6. Hotel
7. Post Office
8. Parking Garage

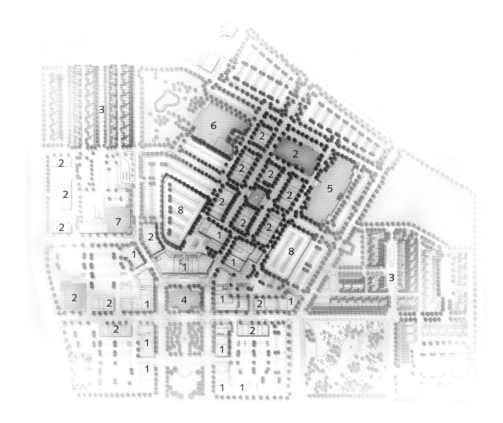

0 100 200 300

By some measures, Southlake Town Square is the most fully realized of the firm's Texas town center and new-community projects. Knitting together national and local retail stores, offices, and civic uses such as a town hall, library, and public parks, it has recently added a townhouse neighborhood. The pedestrian experience here is lively and complex, and there is a sense of place and even permanence.

At the same time, this is something quite different from a locally-grown small town. Attracting a clientele from far beyond the suburban jurisdiction of Southlake, population 25,000, Southlake Town Square has been called a deconstructed regional shopping center—although it does not rely on traditional anchor stores, and is unlike most big shopping centers in fully integrating other uses with retail. As the architects suggest, it might better be seen as a traditional downtown

reconsidered, an old-fashioned grid of walking streets discreetly supercharged with modern levels of surface and structured parking.

Visitors from all over the Dallas-Fort Worth metroplex come here via interstates and suburban arterial roads and head into a system of surface lots, structured parking and on-street parking clearly visible from the site's perimeter. Only then do they leave their cars and step into a world that offers both essential mall merchants from J. Crew to Pottery Barn, and walkable paved squares and green parks, fountains, street trees, arcades, and civic buildings.

As set forth in the architects' 1996 master plan, Southlake Town Square's first phase lines a green civic park with two-story mixed-use buildings. As the setting for the architects' Southlake Town Hall, this space does extra duty by letting passersby see into the project from the existing main arterial road, thereby giving this first group of retail tenants some of the visibility of a strip shopping

center, and marking a clear point of entry for approaching drivers.

An extension of this original, successful critical mass, Grand Avenue branches off at an angle from the Town Hall precinct in a way that suggests a later, more commercial quarter of a traditionally developed small town.

Grand Avenue sets up a second street grid aligned to the north entrance of the 130-acre site. Its design has undergone several changes since the original master plan. Partly because of development economics at the time, Grand Avenue begins near the town hall in a transitional block of two-story mixed-use structures similar in character to the first phase, and then shifts to a new, one-story scale. The architects treat this new condition as a traditional market square that complements and balances the earlier civic square.

Left: Colonnade creates late afternoon play of light and shadow.

Opposite: Small perimeter jets invite a cooling play break at central square fountain.

The style and feeling here resonate with Southwestern and Latin American traditions, following the scheme of a central public market house surrounded by deep, shade-giving colonnades built to the street line, thoroughly appropriate to Texas summers. It is a scheme that also appears in formal neoclassical planning, from Charleston, South Carolina to St. Petersburg, Russia, and the architects honor both classical and vernacular models. As in many older examples that employ one-story buildings at Southlake, tall arches, columns, and parapets give a sense of enclosure to an outdoor space large enough for full-grown trees and a two-tiered fountain.

The modern difference here is that this market square serves an upscale shopping center with individual, identity-conscious national chain retailers. The buildings here are therefore individualized in width and detail. The proportions of the square are determined in part by the background parking structures, surface lots, and parking access paths that make this pedestrian experience possible.

The central structure, which looks to such models as Washington, D.C.'s Georgetown market house of the 1870's, is really two buildings divided by a small plaza, and houses restaurant and retail tenants. Buildings on each side create a spatially continuous street wall, but add varied widths, heights, colors, and materials—primarily synthetic stucco with some brick and cast stone trim—to accommodate varied tenants and a limited budget.

The architects also involved a second Washington, D.C. design firm, Bowie-Gridley Architects, resulting in an even subtler sense of Southlake as a town built and altered by different hands over several decades. A hotel and cinema designed by other architects defines the north edge of Grand Avenue and adds another level of diversity and activity to this successful, new American downtown.

Opposite Top: Four building fronts form one side of the Grand Avenue "market square." Variations in length, parapet height, details, and color identify individual façades within the continuous, block-long arcade.

Opposite Bottom Left: Column, wall, cornice, and parapet are varied along each façade of the arcade.

Opposite Bottom Right: Two-story façades in stucco and brick mark transition between Southlake's Grand Avenue and Town Square districts; see detail this page.

Southlake Townhouses

SOUTHLAKE, TEXAS 2006

Site Plan

0 100 200 300

Seen across the rolling hillside of a two-and-a-half-acre park, with its stand of native trees and gatherings of family dogs, the townhouses known as "The Brownstones at Southlake Town Square" now rival the town hall park as the signature view of the community. Already going beyond the typical suburban market profile for attached houses in the Dallas-Fort Worth metroplex, this is a neighborhood of families and young singles as well as empty nesters and the aging-in-place.

Beginning with the architects' 1996 master plan for Southlake Town Square, the small town of Southlake continues to evolve from an affluent bedroom community with conventional strip shopping centers, toward a place with a mixed-use commercial core, pedestrian-friendly streets, in-town parks, and other civic amenities that have made it a regional destination.

Southlake Town Square's retail and office success sparked interest in a possible residential component from the start—people had literally buttonholed the developer and said, "I'd like to live here." While both architects and developer favored a livable town center, obstacles remained, including not only the original single-use zoning underlying all

of Southlake, but also community skepticism—not unique to Texas—regarding the effect of higher-density housing on surrounding large-lot, single-family real estate values.

A few years later, the community has embraced this first phase of townhouses as a neighborhood on its own terms. It has clearly succeeded as a real estate venture. The first, "beachfront" blocks of row houses facing the site's large park and main approach road, quickly sold on

a lottery basis, leaving a waiting list of over thirty potential buyers for the next phase.

The residential site plan adapts a section of the initial master plan that would have extended the Town Square retail/office grid. Continuing the commercial center's pattern of short, walkable blocks, the revised plan adds alleys to serve garages at the rear of each lot, and an occasional widened street that allows some house fronts to face slender, planted "squares,"

135

Right: End units like this one are entered on the long elevation, here marked with a centered gable and entry porch.

Opposite: Facing park along Summit Avenue, houses are designed as single façades or grouped in pairs and triplets to establish a varied cadence on the street.

like the historic streets of Boston's New South End.

The houses offer subtly modernized adaptations of late Victorian favorites, emphasizing the generous, solid-looking proportions and double-hung windows of H.H. Richardson designs as they were adapted and simplified by pre-World War I builders nationwide. Three models vary based on stairway location and bedroom arrangement, plus bay window options. A fourth, exceptional end unit

design adds a hexagonal corner turret and more windows. In part because regional soil conditions necessitate building without basements, many purchasers have chosen the option of a bonus room above the freestanding rear garage.

Built of several shades of brick with simple brick details and cast stone trim, the rows of housefronts display a calculated balance of style and color variations that draws upon the architects' years of work with historic row houses.

Above: Two octagonal turrets anchor the corners of their respective blocks.

Opposite: Flat-fronted, light-colored façades alternate with red bayfronts to shape a varied streetscape; planting area between house and sidewalk invites individual expression.

In some cases the design groups five or more matching houses, including mirror-image façades, in symmetrical "terraces." Corner buildings and a few other façades are treated as single houses, and elsewhere there are pairs, trios, and quartets of matching designs. Here as in many

138 other projects the architects accomplish stylistic variations with consistent, but rarely obvious, economy; the emphasis is on variations in color and pattern, with extra-cost elements such as sloped roofs and gables applied just enough to give a sense of rich variety. The feeling, rare in modern row house developments, is of a neighborhood assembled over time.

Right: Lined on two sides by housefronts, the two-and-one-half-acre public park preserves the largest stand of native trees within Southlake's 130-acre downtown district.

Below: Three examples of basic three-story, twenty-five foot wide bayfront design show variations in windows, parapets, brick patterns, string courses and other details.

Opposite Below: Townhouse row steps along hillside, paralleling contours of park.

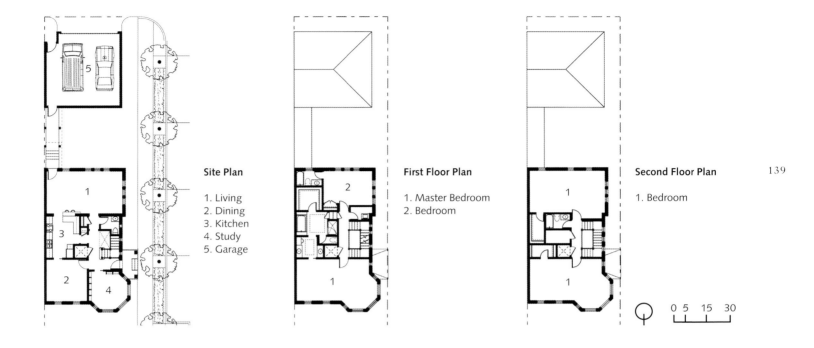

Site Plan

1. Living
2. Dining
3. Kitchen
4. Study
5. Garage

First Floor Plan

1. Master Bedroom
2. Bedroom

Second Floor Plan

1. Bedroom

0 5 15 30

Schermerhorn Symphony Center

NASHVILLE, TENNESSEE   2006

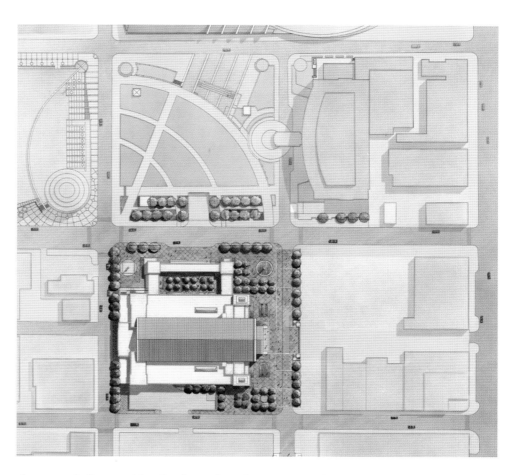

141

"Ah...I get it now."

Denny Bottorff, steering committee chair for the Nashville Symphony's new building project but by his own account no music expert, had reluctantly joined other local leaders and the architects, acousticians, and theater planners on a five-day, five-city visit to seven European concert halls. Dutifully, at first, he had spent three hours on a hard chair listening to the Vienna Philharmonic performing Dvorak's Requiem.

And now, as the last notes faded in the Musikvereinsaal, it all came together. More than acoustical perfection, it was the intimate experience, the sensation of being a participant in a real room, with sunlight filtering through high clerestory windows. Nashville needed this. The Nashville Symphony had been transformed into an ensemble of quality by music director Kenneth Schermerhorn, but was hard to hear in the multipurpose Tennessee Performing Arts Center. The orchestra's Carnegie Hall debut in 2000 had convinced many of the 1,100 attendees from Tennessee that these musicians were better than anyone knew. Now the goal was to bring that experience back home.

Acoustician Paul Scarbrough realized early on that "Music City" has some of the nation's most sophisticated listeners, but with ears tuned to amplified sound. This insight help turn him toward the acoustic immediacy that impressed Bottorff, and a modern realization of a Vienna-style hall. The firm's arrival on the team, influenced by Scarbrough and others who knew the firm's work at Fort Worth's Bass Hall and Cleveland's Severance Hall, reinforced the surprising idea that the old "shoebox" shape, with windows, exposed ceiling and all, could work in a modern building.

Selection of a site fronting Gateway Park in the developing SoBro (South of Broadway) district led to another surprise: the architect's conclusion that the

Opposite: The ceremonial north portico opens its doors in preparation for a festive evening event.

Below: North portico overlooks pedestrian street, foreground, leading from Gateway Park to Cumberland River.

Following Pages: North façade conveys classical dignity with unusual degree of transparency and openness; this view from future Broadway approach shows Orpheus and Eurydice pediment by sculptor Raymond Kaskey.

hall's formal entrance portico should face a yet-to-be-developed pedestrian connection to Broadway, and that a garden

144

front—pavilions, colonnade, terrace, and Viennese café—should face the grassy park. As built, the garden terrace entices visitors from the adjacent Country Music Hall of Fame with a ticket office, tours, classes, and café lunches. Meanwhile the main portico steps provide a grandstand for the pedestrian street that leads to the Cumberland River bridge two blocks away.

Filling a city block, the Symphony Center surrounds the 1900-seat Laura Turner Concert Hall with a rectangular doughnut—separated from the hall by a continuous acoustical isolation joint—of circulation, function rooms, and support spaces.

Both circulation spaces and exterior employ Beaux-Arts planning while staying close to early 19th century neoclassical proportions, natural in a city famed for Greek Revival landmarks and long known as the Athens of the South. As with such traditional halls as Schinkel's 1818 Schauspielhaus in Berlin, the limestone and granite exterior is a rational expression of the spaces within, with a classical portico as the symbolic focus. Its columns, like many throughout the building, adapt 19th century architect William Strickland's local Egyptian variation on the Greek Doric order, including capitals decorated with iris buds. Their resemblance to riverboat smokestacks is incidental but not inappropriate. The well-known figurative sculptor

Ray Kaskey created the pediment group, a powerful modern-realist retelling of the Orpheus legend.

The main lobby's light-beige, two-story balconied space brings the portico's giant order indoors. Sparingly decorated with the elegant globe chandeliers, metal railings and marble floors found throughout the building, this room is a Tennessee antebellum mansion turned inside out.

Side lobbies flanking the concert hall are long and skylit, with two tiers of columns and balconies sized for intermission crowds and refreshments. The west lobby opens to the low main café and, in warm weather, the intimately

Above Left: Facing Gateway Park, colonnade and garden terrace enliven west side approach with public, daytime activities, including box office, tours, stage door, and café with outdoor seating.

Above: South façade, enclosing backstage area and other back-of-house functions, displays high level of architectural detail, anticipating pedestrian-oriented development envisioned in area master plan.

Far Left: West tower turns corner from ceremonial to garden front, provides one of two main street level entries for varied programs and events.

Left: Seen through streetside colonnade, garden terrace attracts tourists and local visitors, while providing café seating and outdoor function space.

downscaled terrace and colonnade facing the park. On the floor above the Founders Room and Green Room can accommodate a variety of functions, with cherry-like African makore paneling, French, Russian, English and Biedermeyer antiques. Upper tier ticket buyers receive the same level of finish as the box holders below, with the added richness of lobby ceilings with decorative plaster vaults.

Ornamental programs in a variety of stone, metal, and wood media enrich the building and its interiors. The main themes are the Tennessee state flowers, iris and passionflower, and musical motifs such as staffs, G-clefs, keyboards, and lyres.

Laura Turner Hall follows the shoebox formula with an orchestra level and boxes, a grand tier of second level boxes (available on performance nights if subscribers decline to use them) and balcony, and a similar upper tier. Above this the clerestory, with its acoustically engineered double layer windows, forms a lightly scaled colonnade at the top of the room, visually supporting the coffered ceiling.

Equally attracted to a raked floor with comfortable fixed seats and good sightlines, and a flat floor adaptable to pops concerts, balls and other events, the

Left: A half-level above street, north main lobby continues giant order of main entrance portico in grand gathering space.

Opposite: One of two main ceremonial stairs, West tower's grand stair shows rich use of metal and stone.

148

sponsors found a way to have both. In a system unique to Nashville, eight 30,000 pound "wagons" of raked, fixed seats roll forward and drop into the basement via hydraulic lift, leaving a flat floor. Each transformation takes a small crew about an hour and a half.

The Vienna-inspired stage backdrop is an enormous organ case and choral loft with additional stage risers below. Makore woodwork and Brazilian cherry floors include "Old Hickory" inlays honoring Nashville's adoptive son, Andrew Jackson. The red stage and floor contrast with the multiple shades of off-white and celadon of the walls and ceilings. These recede and project in multilayer, multicolor coffers and panels like French-matted picture frames—at once acoustical design and interior architecture.

The acoustical engineers used a large architectural model to test a variety of precisely calculated surface treatments before arriving at the current, adjustable system. Fabric banners and fabric wrapped panels are employed to achieve the variable acoustics required to accommodate both amplified and acoustical performances. As in older halls, relief decorations on balcony fronts create

Left: Window opposite west tower stair landing connects upper lobby with a view of Gateway Park. Tennessee iris motif reappears in metalwork shown here and on opposite page.

Opposite: East and west lobbies enable natural light to penetrate from skylights and laylights (photo upper right) to founders (box) level and orchestra low level. Photos far left and lower right show two-level colonnades.

diffuse reflections of high frequency sound waves. The design here is a small memoir of the concert hall donors' mother, Laura Turner, depicting a stylized piano keyboard, roses and tulips, pony heads, and a horseshoe.

To its affinities with the concert-going experience of the past, the Symphony Center adds a positive difference in its sense of lightness and openness to the city. It is an accurate architectural expression of a program that includes a full time

education center, community outreach programs, tours, and a variety of events beyond symphony performances. In the inclusive spirit of Kenneth Schermerhorn, who died a little more than a year before its opening, this is a place that, in Denny Bottorff's words, belongs not just to the community but "to everybody in the community, individually."

Above Left: Founders Room, with African makore paneling, can be combined with Green Room for receptions and other functions.

Left: Green Room's engaged columns repeat main lobby order. Antique and reproduction furniture complement both Nashville traditions and modern neoclassical architecture.

Opposite: Balcony lobby illustrates this public building's egalitarian nature: founders level finishes are more elaborate, but vaulted space, light and views are special rewards for upper balcony patrons.

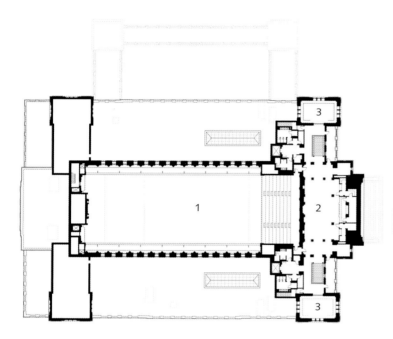

Balcony High Level Plan

1. Concert Hall
2. Lobby
3. Open to Below

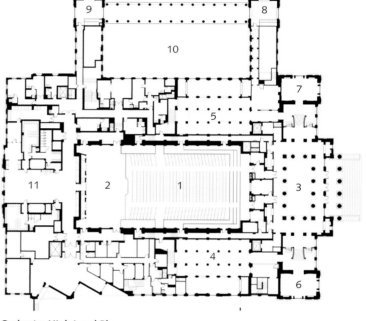

Orchestra High Level Plan

1. Concert Hall
2. Concert Platform
3. Main Lobby
4. East Lobby
5. West Lobby
6. East Entry
7. West Entry
8. Box Office
9. Stage Door Entry
10. Courtyard
11. Orchestra Lounge

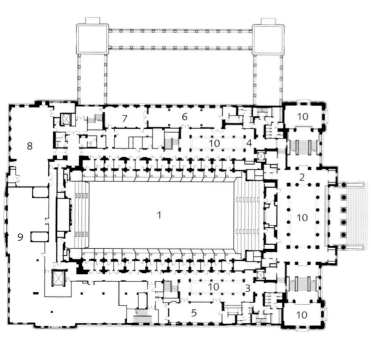

Founders Level Plan

1. Concert Hall
2. Main Lobby
3. East Lobby
4. West Lobby
5. Board Room
6. Founders Room
7. Green Room
8. Education Room
9. Administrative Offices
10. Open to Below

0 10 20   40

Following Pages: The Laura Turner Concert Hall, here in full 1,900 seat configuration, reinterprets the shoebox form and clerestory lighting of historic halls using modern materials and technologies.

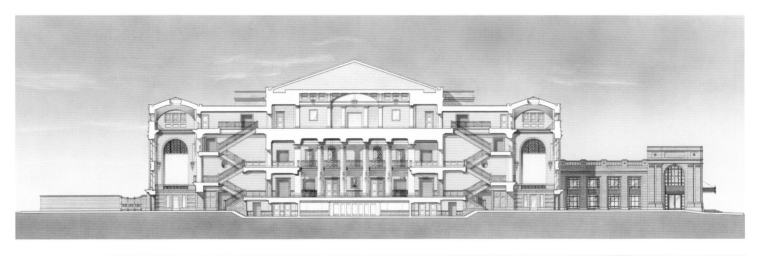

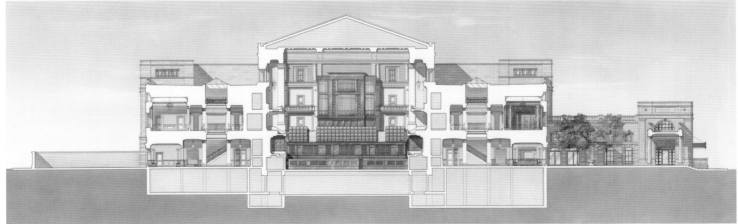

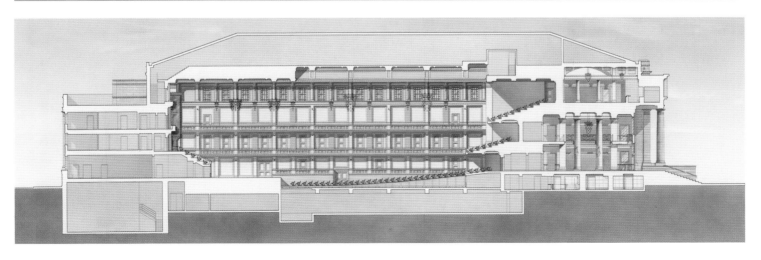

156

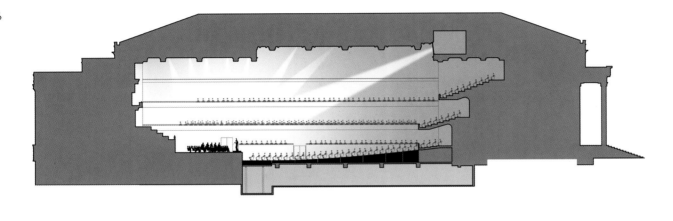

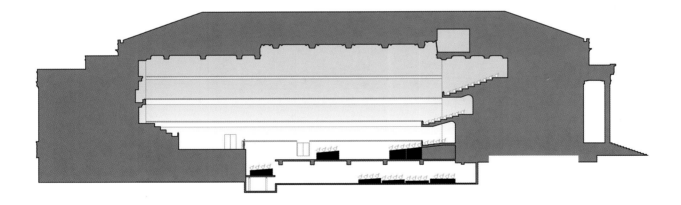

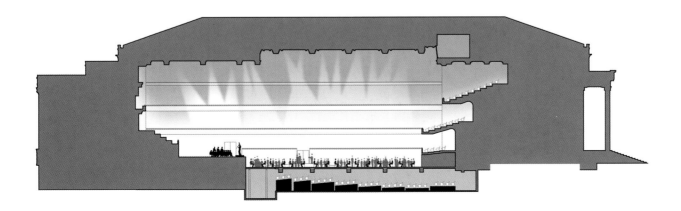

0 5 10 20 30

Above and Opposite: The hall can be trasformed from a traditional raked floor auditorium with 1,000 fixed theater seats at orchestra level (top figure) to a 6,000 square foot flat floor suitable for cabaret style seating and other uses compatible with a ball room (bottom figure). The raked orchestra floor is comprised of eight movable chair wagons. As shown in the center figure, the wagon can be moved automatically one by one from the hall to a lift in front of the stage. The lift lowers the basement level and each wagon is offloaded to a storage room immediately under the hall. The sequence is reversed to change the room back for orchestral concerts. The changeover takes just under two hours to go from one arrangement to the other.

Left: View from chorus seats—sometimes available to concert patrons—shows balconies at rear of auditorium.

Opposite: A founders tier box overlooks the concert platform and organ case, both detailed with African makore wood paneling. Organ grill ornament includes iris and flying lyre motifs.

160

Left and Opposite: Concert stage grillwork and paneling contribute to acoustic design, as do recessed wall and soffit panels and bas-relief ornament of balcony fronts.

Sid Richardson Museum

FORT WORTH, TEXAS 2006

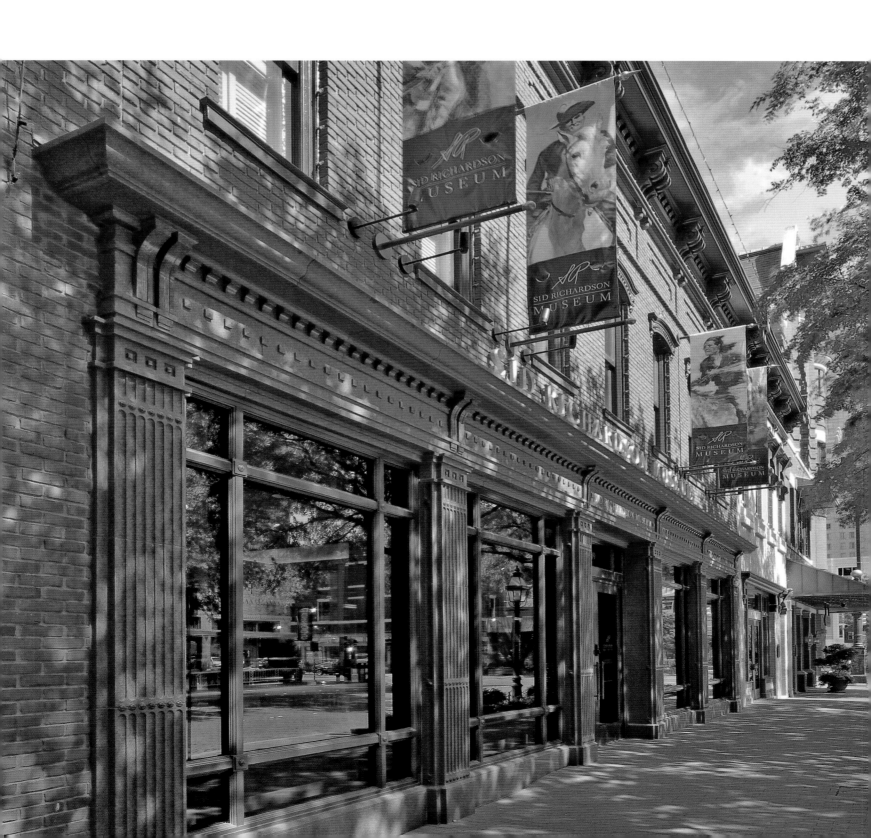

The Sid Richardson Museum houses an exemplary collection of Western art—emphasizing early 20th century paintings by Frederic Remington and Charles Russell—behind what at first looks like a Victorian storefront on Fort Worth's historic Main Street.

In reality, the original 1895 commercial building was demolished long ago, replaced with a building that combined a reproduction of the original on the upper levels with a late 1970's entry façade. For the renovation, the firm resolved to kept the upper levels intact while replacing the ground floor façade with a reimagination of the original design, but in monumental materials worthy of the civic purpose of the Museum.

The new front in finely detailed red granite and bronze conveys explicitly that this is a public institution, distinct from its commercial neighbors. The difference appears in details like the cast bronze "buffalo nickels" that decorate the granite columns, in place of the generic neo-grec rosettes found on old sheet metal storefronts. More generally, the architects' attention to the sidewalk experience, also seen in the Tarrant County Family Law Center and Bank One buildings nearby, supports pedestrian values in a car-bound city.

Sid W. Richardson, the oilman and rancher who died in 1959, started his Western art collection in the 1940's, in friendly competition with publisher-oilman Amon Carter.

Carter wanted a place for his artworks in Fort Worth's Cultural District with a view of the city skyline, an idea later realized in a Philip Johnson-designed pavilion and garden with many subsequent additions. Richardson's collection

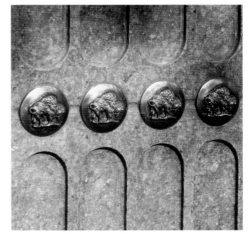

Above: On-street windows add to museum's visibility.

Right: Detail of fluted pilasters shows cast-bronze "buffalo nickel" rosettes.

Opposite: Materials and details distinguish Sid Richardson Museum as public building among commercial fronts of Sundance Square.

164 opened to the public at its current Main Street address, below the unassuming headquarters of the Sid W. Richardson Foundation, in 1989. It rubs shoulders with a former drover's hotel and a one-time poker palace, establishments Remington and Russell might have visited on their way to record the disappearing frontier.

Appropriately, the current, extensive redesign maintains a special balance of cowtown commerce and artistic gravity.

On the casual side, there is not only a storefront but also a store to attract passersby. Four columns that reproduce cast iron originals are the only separation between the museum shop and the reception lobby. The remodeling also

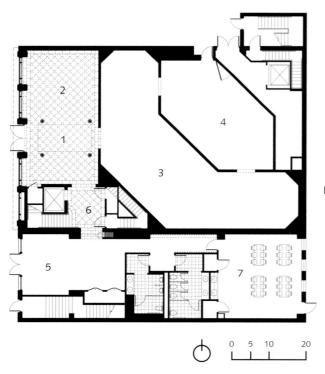

First Floor Plan

1. Museum Lobby
2. Gift Shop
3. Exhibit Area:
   Front Gallery
4. Exhibit Area:
   Diamond Gallery
5. Group Entry
6. Elevator Lobby
7. Education Room

0 5 10 20

Above Left: Metal columns, recreating those found in original 1890's commercial interior, here define the path from street entrance to gallery entrance in open lobby. Continuous French limestone floors, minimal details help maintain focus on artworks.

Left: Finish treatment of initial exhibition in front gallery highlights a tryptich of paintings.

Above: Gallery space division accommodates rotating shows, with wing-shaped front gallery and smaller, diamond-shaped inner gallery (through opening) offering display alternatives. Moveable walls, lighting enable other configurations (note different openings in floor plan opposite).

Opposite Above: Accent wall color was added to the diamond gallery to complement Remington's famed group of Nocturnes.

Opposite Below: View from diamond gallery to front gallery.

incorporates a small adjacent building to add a second entry and a classroom for school groups. Nearby, a Peter Hurd portrait of Sid Richardson on his ranch, with accompanying quote, reassures visitors that this is a genuinely personal collection.

On the artistic side, the two galleries beyond represent a rethinking of how best to show the Richardson collection, based in part on a National Gallery of Art exhibition that borrowed several

of the paintings and displayed them in ways that suggested some of the changes made here.

In contrast to the Old West connotations of the storefront and shop, the carpeted gallery spaces are neutral and modern, emphasizing these artists' painterly skill over their links to time and place. The architects reconfigured the existing space as a lozenge-shaped inner gallery with a large, wing-shaped outer gallery wrapping around it. The diagonal

Above Left: Corridor leading to classroom doubles as a staging area with cubbies, coathooks.

Above: Mosaic tile friezes of bison animate restrooms.

Opposite: Two views from second floor reception area show renovated office space shared by the museum and the Foundation.

geometry and minimal, squared-off reveals at baseboards and door openings recall the large, lower level addition to Paris's Marmottan Museum, with its single, long line of Monets.

The new galleries provide a previously unrealized flexibility. The remodeled space incorporates changeable openings and adaptable partitions that allow the Museum to expand the collection and create focus exhibits. With an eye toward these goals, the design team pre-programmed several future exhibits.

A new installation, the artworks are hung more selectively than in the past, in simple, early-20th-century frames. Colored walls complement some groups of paintings, notably a selection of the famous Nocturnes, the twilight and moonlight pictures that cemented Remington's critical reputation near the end of his career.

Parker Square Buildings

FLOWER MOUND, TEXAS 2006

Site Plan

0   200

Parker Square was to have been a conventional suburban office park: a loop road with three large office buildings, plus smaller, pad-site retail and restaurant structures amid surface parking. In 1996 the firm began to work with a new owner and the city of Flower Mound, Texas, on a different planning and zoning concept for these twenty-four acres: two-story mixed-use buildings lining two perpendicular, walkable streets, parking in the rear, and a green town square facing Cross Timbers Road, the area's main artery.

Comprising about 350,000 square feet, Parker Square is a neighborhood center rather than a town center. Its storefronts are carefully detailed but narrow and modest compared to the national franchise stores at nearby Southlake. Representing local vernacular styles, they fit the restaurants and shops that serve office tenants on site, plus neighbors from Flower Mound and nearby Lewisville. Curb appeal matters here, however, since these retailers need to attract traffic from the main road without help from an anchor store. The square and several architectural eye-catchers at the street corners support this, and the buildings glimpsed at the end of each street complete the attractive picture.

These two street-ending buildings, by their relatively large size, prominent sites, and ambitious architecture, suggest a civic purpose. Privately owned, both were planned for public roles from the beginning.

Closing Parker Square's north-south axis, the 55,000 square foot Health and Athletic Center combines a health club plus 20,000 square feet of commercial office space. In the rear the site slopes down to parkland and a jogging path, helping to make this as much an informal neighborhood center as a private club. The lobby atrium inside accommodates various level changes and showcases the club's many offerings, from weight rooms to a lap pool.

A mansard roof and a first floor set below street level disguise the Center's three-story height, enabling the stadium-like front elevation of tall Roman arches recessed entry, below the gallery of closely spaced windows that marks the office floor. The red brick façade bristles with pumped-up imagery: rustications, crenellations, exposed steel roof scuppers, Texas Lone Stars in metal and cast stone, and a brick frieze of stylized barbells.

At the corresponding end of Parker Square's east-west street, the development's largest commercial office building was designed to serve the image of local government tenants as well as the area Chamber of Commerce. A two-column, in-antis portico in buff brick and limestone creates a focus for the street, using its deeply recessed entrance for strong graphic effect. The portico's low gabled parapet with bull's-eye window is a calculated choice, suggesting civic importance without the grandeur of a classical pediment. The symmetrical wings look to French Beaux-Arts precedents, with classicizing detail but modern, wide bays.

Below: The building's classically ordered façade and image of dignified permanence fits its role as home to area chamber of commerce and local government offices.

Opposite: Portico is designed as focal point for end of main east-west street.

170

A third new mixed-use building is commercial in function and character, but also plays a civic part with respect to urban design. With its long, multi-storefront elevation on Cross Timbers Road, and drum-like turret at the turn-in to Parker Square, this is a grander and more urbane building than its neighbors. An adjacent, contrasting façade, actually part of the same new building, makes a careful transition to the humbler storefronts up the street. The turret and its first floor porch, banks of large windows, brown iron spot brick, and highly stylized classicizing, light-colored cast stone detail are all gestures to motorists, a visual invitation to take part in a pedestrian environment.

Parker Square's master plan envisions several more buildings along Cross Timbers Road. Two, both triangular in plan, would complete a four-sided enclosure of the green square, while maintaining attractive views of the interior for passing motorists. Here as in the architects' other neighborhood and town center plans, the goal of a driver-friendly perception from the outside, and a pedestrian-friendly experience from the inside, is achieved with remarkably little compromise.

Above Left: Vertical piers and pair of arched windows emphasize the center of this forty foot commercial front near the entrance to Parker Square.

Left: Compared to the narrower façades within the project, buildings turn their long face to the main arterial road.

Opposite: Engaged drum with columned base marks primary Parker Sqaure entrance.

172

Above: Occupying a full block at terminus of Parker Square's main north-south street, health club and office building open to community parkland. Architecture suggests civic role of a sports facility.

Left: Accessible entrance ramps are discreetly incorporated within a deep entrance arcade. Crenellated parapet above integrates row of office windows.

Opposite: Details expressing physical strength and civic purpose include brick corbels, deep-set windows under exposed steel lintels, functional steel scuppers, and brick barbell frieze.

Private Residence

NEW ENGLAND 2007

Site Plan

1. Main House
2. Guest House
3. Garage

0 40 80 120

This summer cottage represents an understanding more than a replication of the Shingle Style, the "architecture of the American summer" defined by David Schwarz's longtime mentor, architectural historian Vincent Scully. Along with the Gilded Age romance the style evokes, the architects here recall its origins in the spare Stick Style cottages of the 1870's, and its successors in the long-lined Prairie Style and Arts and Crafts designs of the early 20th century.

Open meadow and woodland cover most of the nine-acre property, surrounded by conservation land and oceanfront. The main building site commands some 270 degrees of water views. On its south side the 7,500 square foot main house and a 900 square foot, one-bedroom guest house, equipped with a ship's ladder and loft for overflow guests, shelter the swimming pool with its stone-paved terrace and garden beyond. A third structure, a three-car garage with an exercise room above, sits some distance away near the edge of the woods.

A walk around the buildings, all cedar-shingled with concise gray trim and stone water tables, offers subtly changing perspectives, at times suggesting the multi-gable roofscape of a small village.

It may come as a surprise, then, to learn that the roof peaks—the long main ridge, and the tops of the many shorter cross axes and bays or "ells"—are all roughly

Opposite: Above the main entry porch, tall windows light the window seat niche of the library between the guest wing, left, and master suite, right.

the same height, about twenty-seven feet above first floor level. Disguised by multiple gables, shed dormers and other details that break the overall mass into smaller parts, this literal low profile stems from local building restrictions, and the owners' desire to subordinate the house to the land. In contrast to the dramatic crags favored by Victorian seaside resorts, parts of the site here were actually lowered somewhat to achieve the required overall elevation.

Inside, the many gable ends enable a range of second-floor, slope-ceilinged volumes with a variety of generous, mostly double-hung or transom windows. Two identical gabled axes, each one oriented to an equally dramatic water view, intersect to form the twenty-five foot high, wood-ceilinged cross vault of the Great Room. This is the house's gathering place and spatial climax, with an adjoining open kitchen and dining porch beyond.

Paralleling the long roof ridge visible above he entrance, a circulation spine organizes the floor plan. On the first floor it takes the form of a Shingle Style living hall, with a main entrance off the front

porch and a spindled, paneled staircase. From here the Great Room lies straight ahead beyond the mass of the main chimney.

To the right, the owner's wing includes a mud room entrance off the porte cochere, a sun room and study on the first floor, and a master bedroom suite and roof deck on the floor above. With the rest of the house closed off, this wing including the kitchen can function as an independent "sub-house" in the off-season.

To the left of the entry hall, a separate two-story wing provides seasonal accommodations for the owner's four grown children and their families, plus guests. Reachable by a second stair with lighthouse newel post, the choices include bedrooms, a children's nautical bunk-room, and a sleeping porch.

In lieu of a second floor hallway linking the owner's wing and children's wing, the space above the entry hall offers a traditional library, with a fireplace, window seat, and coved ceiling. The full height American walnut paneling here again combines Shingle Style precedents with

176

freshly designed, technologically current detailing. A smaller teak-paneled study reflects a similar approach.

Like the original Shingle Style houses built along the New England coast, this summer place adapts the forms of traditional local cottages, barns and other utilitarian structures to an informal, family-oriented, modern vacation lifestyle. The Great Room with its open kitchen and high, cross-vaulted living-dining space has no close precedent in the late 19th century. Instead, this summer cottage honors the inventive spirit that produced the pioneering open plans of the Shingle Style era, with its own new-old openness for the 21st century.

Above: West front porches embrace entry drive.

Left: South side of main house overlooks pool terrace and sunken garden; dining porch, at right of house, commands ocean view.

Opposite, Top: Approached from the south, the guest house, left, and main house appear beyond a field of tall grass.

Opposite, Bottom: Beyond the main entry at far right in photo, the curved porch signals the location of the guest wing.

Following Pages: View from pond of the north side of main house, showing use of gables ends to break up visual mass.

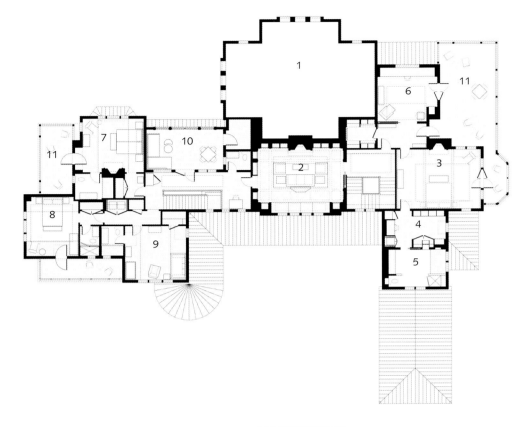

Second Floor Plan

1. Great Room Below
2. Library
3. Master Bedroom
4. Dressing
5. Master Bathroom
6. Study
7. Botanical Room
8. Ocean Room
9. Nursery
10. Sleeping Porch
11. Deck

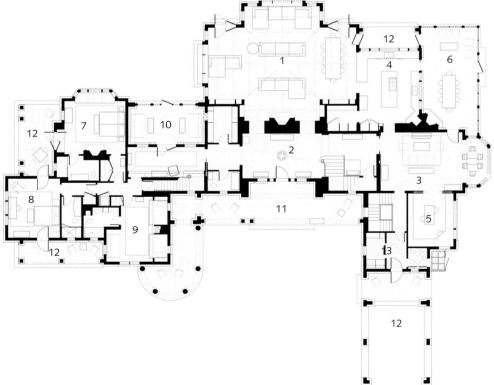

First Floor Plan

1. Great Room
2. Entry Hall
3. Sunroom
4. Kitchen
5. Study
6. Screened Dining Porch
7. Shell Room
8. President's Room
9. Grand Kid's Bunk Room
10. Guest Porch
11. Entry Porch
12. Car Port
13. Mud Room

Opposite: The Great Room, focal space of the main house, offers both pond views (windows at left) and ocean views (windows at right). Cross-vault ceiling is finished in beaded maple. Table in foreground adjoins open kitchen.

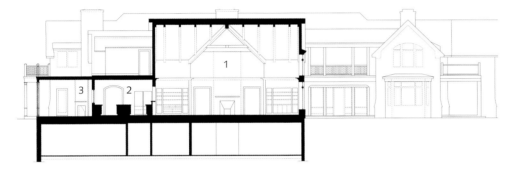

Section Looking West

1. Great Room
2. Kitchen
3. Screened Dining Porch

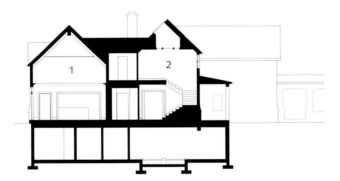

Section Looking South

1. Guest Porch
2. Main Stair Hall

0 2 4   8

Opposite and Left: The main entry hall recalls a traditional Shingle Style living hall with herringbone-patterned maple paneling, fluted pilasters, spindled stair railings, and bracketed ceiling beams. Smaller photo looks toward guest wing with front door at left, Great Room at right.

184

Above: Dining corner of Great Room opens to kitchen and dining porch beyond.

Opposite: Screened dining porch provides generous space and ocean views.

Above and Opposite: Library serves as a quiet gathering place and a link between second floor family/guest bedrooms and master suite. Detail at right shows window seat, box-pattern walnut paneling between fluted pilasters, coffered wood soffit surrounding plaster ceiling cove.

Left: Designed by the architects, lighthouse newel post identifies guest wing stair and way to children's bedrooms.

Above: A guest bedroom occupies one of main house's many gabled spaces.

Opposite: Beneath vaulted, maple-paneled ceiling, master bedroom opens to private roof decks and panoramic sea view.

Above: Guest house and porte cochere, at right, shelter pool terrace from north and west winds.

Opposite: Paneled in beaded maple, guest house living area incorporates a ship's ladder to loft above.

Chapman Cultural Center

SPARTANBURG, SOUTH CAROLINA 2007

200 EAST ST. JOHN STREET

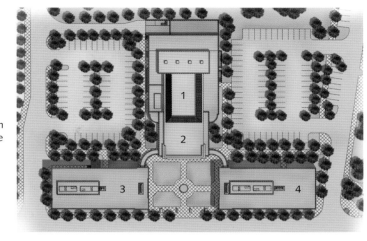

Site Plan

1. 500-Seat Theater
2. Main Lobby
3. Art & History Museum
4. Ballet School & Science Center

0   50   100

Once known as "the Lowell of the South" for its water-powered cotton mills, Spartanburg, South Carolina remains a textile center that also makes chemical products and BMW's. With adjacent Greenville as a constant competitor, Spartanburg has remade its historic downtown and organized its cultural assets to promote a distinctive identity.

The Chapman Cultural Center realizes the dream of the Arts Partnership of Greater Spartanburg, which in 1990 brought together eight organizations including art and science museums, performing arts institutions, studio artists, and schools. Led by textile executive W. Marshall Chapman, the partnership concluded that these programs would thrive through interaction in a new center; that a united facility would improve regional visibility; and that a successful new center could anchor an expansion of Spartanburg's revitalized downtown.

After meeting the terms of a $16.5 million challenge grant from four local families, by 2002 fundraisers needed more money for a 112,000-square-foot, $36 million building proposed for Barnet Park at the edge of downtown. As new contributors pitched in and the partnership hired a new project manager, the firm became involved and was asked to study a more affordable design.

The architects discovered that most of the center's requirements—galleries, exhibit halls, studios, and classrooms—could be housed in relatively economical loft space. It was primarily the 500-seat multipurpose theater that demanded special life safety and fire protection provisions, mechanical systems, acoustical details and the like. Placing these two different types of uses in adjacent but separate buildings could save money on construction, and enable a phased master plan, with relatively easy

expansion in keeping with later priorities and funding.

Inaugurated in 2007, the first-phase Chapman Cultural Center comprises 86,000 gross square feet, at a cost of $27 million.

The center occupies a newly selected five-acre site donated by the city, still adjacent to Barnet Park but closer to downtown as a gesture to new development. The three initial buildings define a wall on busy St. John Street. The limestone-clad theater building is set back from the twin brick-faced museum/studio buildings to define the brick-and-limestone entrance plaza, designed

Below: Chapman Cultural Center's three initial buildings enclose a south-facing plaza oriented toward downtown Spartanburg.

Opposite: Planned as the centerpiece of the future arts campus, the limestone theater building alludes to city's historic Greek Revival architecture.

193

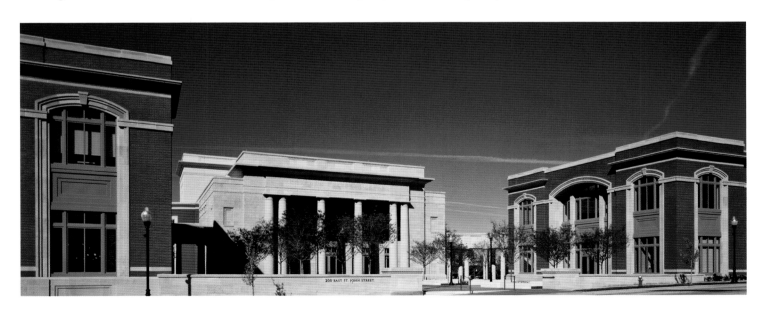

with landscape architect Michael Verga-son. The master plan envisions a second phase of two-story loftlike buildings on St. John Street enclosing an expanded parking area, and a grid of small streets serving an eventual dense, walkable arts campus.

The three completed structures combine a number of practical solutions and cultural allusions. Related to the stylish industrial lofts once built by affluent manufacturers in Spartanburg and other U.S. cities, the brick buildings derive from late 19th century efforts by French Beaux-Arts designers to reconcile the wide spans and large windows of utilitarian metal construction with the civic language of neoclassicism. Adopting the French idea of wide stone-trimmed segmental arches and tall, verdigris-finished metal windows creates a light-filled but formal façade, and these elevations follow that model. The theater, which provides the lobby and function space for the entire center, employs a grander entrance of limestone columns, but

its cornice and entablature match the lines of the adjacent buildings and its details are similarly stylized and pared down. Here the reference is to the spare neoclassicism found in many early 19th century European theaters, and to the Greek Revival typical of the American piedmont.

Low quarter-circle pergolas connect the side buildings to the two-story main lobby, where tall doors and windows open to the portico and plaza. A terrazzo floor, coffered ceiling with varied lighting options, and a long balcony with grand stairways at each end make this a versatile space for public functions.

Beyond a row of paired columns, the theater provides a two-level horseshoe of parterre and balcony seating. The stepped, circular dome above incorporates lighting and air handling equipment below a central stained-glass laylight in a compass rose design. Almost all finishes are simple gypsum board and paint. The theater with its proscenium

Above: Loft buildings create a rhythmic edge along St. John Street.

Opposite Top: Movable walls shape an exhibition within a Spartanburg Museum of Art loft space.

Opposite Below Left: Spartanburg History Museum employs exposed wood trusses in its space on loft building's second floor.

Opposite Below Right: Tall windows light an informal children's classroom in the Science Center.

stage is intimate enough for one-person acoustical concerts, but has a fly loft, orchestra pit, and support spaces that allow fully-staged musical theater and chamber opera productions.

Each of the two-story loft buildings has its own two-story windowed lobby facing the plaza; a side entrance toward the parking areas; and skylit central corridors, that divide the floors into small and large spaces. Larger exhibition and studio areas leave the high ceilings and their structural elements exposed. Even in the simplest spaces, the wide, tall segmental-arch windows add a feeling of civic importance, and a visual connection to the park and surrounding city.

The Chapman Cultural Center has proved to be a source of civic pride and a catalyst for downtown activity as hoped. It also offers a case study of an alternative for cultural facility development: neither baroque sculptural monument, nor bohemian adaptive use on a shoestring budget, but something in between, with flexibility and dignity.

Above: The building's brick and limestone are tarried into the plaza paving. A combination of trees, benches, and grass provide opportunities for smaller gatherings in a shaded setting.

Opposite: Theater's grand lobby and limestone portico open directly to plaza, encouraging accessible, indoor-outdoor functions; change in paving articulates edge of portico.

Left and Below: The grand lobby serves theater performances, cultural center events, and other civic functions. Patterned terrazzo floors and other surfaces in cream, beige and green provide a flexible, durable backdrop for all occasions. Large glass areas enliven the interior and invite use of outdoor spaces.

Opposite: Theater building corner displays sharp lines of Indiana limestone detailing. Quarter-circle pergolas, as seen at right, link theater to the two flanking loft buildings.

200

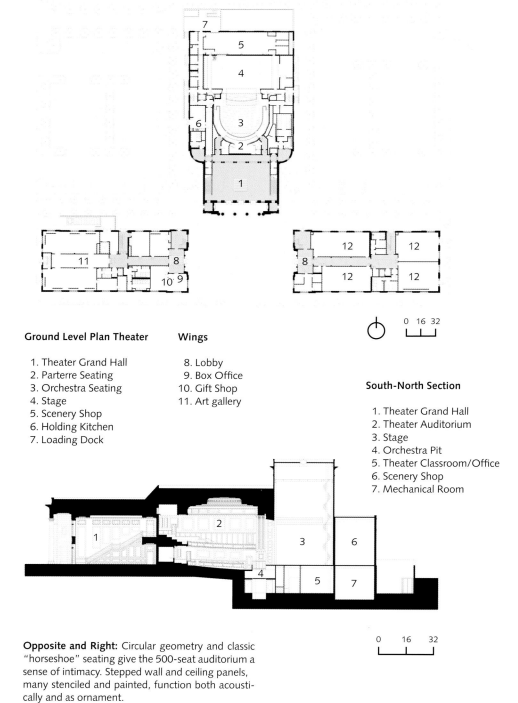

Ground Level Plan Theater

1. Theater Grand Hall
2. Parterre Seating
3. Orchestra Seating
4. Stage
5. Scenery Shop
6. Holding Kitchen
7. Loading Dock

Wings

8. Lobby
9. Box Office
10. Gift Shop
11. Art gallery

0 16 32

South-North Section

1. Theater Grand Hall
2. Theater Auditorium
3. Stage
4. Orchestra Pit
5. Theater Classroom/Office
6. Scenery Shop
7. Mechanical Room

0 16 32

Opposite and Right: Circular geometry and classic "horseshoe" seating give the 500-seat auditorium a sense of intimacy. Stepped wall and ceiling panels, many stenciled and painted, function both acoustically and as ornament.

Opposite and Right: The theater's proscenium arch frames a flexible stage that can accommodate everything from solo recitals to fully-staged musicals. Subtle color palette reinforces a sense of civic dignity.

Bibliography

2002–2008

PUBLICATIONS
2002–2008

DATE	PUBLICATION/ARTICLE	SUBJECT
01/28/08	*New York Times* "Texas Ensemble Plants Flag in New York"	Bass Performance Hall
01/26/08	*Spartanburg Herald-Journal* "Clinton plays overtime gig at Chapman Center event"	Chapman Cultural Center
01/25/08	*Fort Worth Star-Telegram* "Topping out at top of office market"	Carnegie Building
01/25/08	*Spartanburg Herald-Journal* "Bill Clinton campaigns for his wife at Chapman Center event"	Chapman Cultural Center
01/24/08	*Spartanburg Herald-Journal* "Bill Clinton at Chapman Center in Spartanburg Friday"	Chapman Cultural Center
12/30/07	*Spartanburg Herald-Journal* "Chapman Cultural Center"	Chapman Cultural Center
12/27/07	*Spartanburg Herald-Journal* "City looks back at progressive year, strides forward with '08 projects"	Chapman Cultural Center
12/18/07	*Spartanburg Herald-Journal* "Yellow Pages features cultural center on cover"	Chapman Cultural Center
12/17/07	*Spartanburg Herald-Journal* "Chapman Center featured on new phone book"	Chapman Cultural Center
10/25/07	*Las Vegas SUN* Editorial: Building the arts "Progress on performing arts center should encourage more community support"	The Smith Center for the Performing Arts
10/24/07	*Las Vegas SUN* "Arts center to mix it up: 'Eclectic' architect's test: Make an impression in Vegas"	The Smith Center for the Performing Arts

10/23/07	*Spartanburg Herald-Journal* "Repertory Company makes CCC new home for new season"	Chapman Cultural Center
10/04/07	*Spartanburg Herald-Journal* "Spartanburg rejoices in realization of downtown dream"	Chapman Cultural Center
10/03/07	*Spartanburg Herald-Journal* "By day's end, Spartanburg will again have a Downtown home for the arts"	Chapman Cultural Center
10/02/07	*Spartanburg Herald-Journal* (Supplement) "Chapman Cultural Center Community Guide"	Chapman Cultural Center
09/28/07	*Spartanburg Herald-Journal* "Full day planned for Chapman grand opening"	Chapman Cultural Center
09/18/07	*Spartanburg Herald-Journal* "Venue change gives drama group new options"	Chapman Cultural Center
08/09/07	*Las Vegas SUN* "A performing arts center will have a transforming effect on Southern Nevada"	The Smith Center for the Performing Arts
07/29/07	*Spartanburg Herald-Journal* "Designs on the future"	Chapman Cultural Center
04/24/07	*Spartanburg Herald-Journal* "Spartanburg Art Museum gets new logo, locale"	Chapman Cultural Center
Winter '07	*The College*—The Magazine for Alumni of St. John's College, Annapolis, MD	David Schwarz Profile
03/24/07	*Spartanburg Herald-Journal* "Construction still on schedule for site"	Chapman Cultural Center
03/10/07	*Toronto Star* "Palace of culture in land of country music; 'Nashville's new concert hall a gem'"	Schermerhorn Symphony Center
01/24/07	*Houston Chronicle* "Allen House, long a local residential icon, will soon be gone, replaced by a mixed-use project of housing, offices and retail"	Regent Square

01/16/07	*The Plain Dealer* "Nashville's new center: classic in country's home"	Schermerhorn Symphony Center
01/14/07	*The Tennessean* "Cleveland Orchestra visit a highlight for new concert hall"	Schermerhorn Symphony Center
11/01/06	*Indianapolis Star* "Model for area's only 'true concert hall' unveiled" "Carmel residents weigh in on center"	Carmel Regional Performing Arts Center
10/31/06	*Indianapolis Star* "Carmel arts hall to put on the ritz if the donors pony up"	Carmel Regional Performing Arts Center
10/19/06	*Washington Post* "Rhapsody in Orange"	Schermerhorn Symphony Center
10/13/06	*Las Vegas SUN* ARTS NOTES: "Smith Center design team"	The Smith Center for the Performing Arts
Sep./Oct. '06	*Symphony Magazine* "Let There Be Light: 'Through their transparent and open designs, new concert halls are reflecting the ways orchestras interact with the community'"	Schermerhorn Symphony Center
09/18–24/06	*Variety* "Nashville Nights"	Schermerhorn Symphony Center
09/17/06	*Birmingham News* "Nashville boasts new, near-perfect symphony hall"	Schermerhorn Symphony Center
09/12/06	*Wall Street Journal* "Nashville Goes Classical"	Schermerhorn Symphony Center
09/12/06	*Memphis Commercial Appeal* "Schermerhorn Center has Old World Character"	Schermerhorn Symphony Center
09/11/06	*New York Times* "Music City's Music Hall: Orpheus Says Howdy"	Schermerhorn Symphony Center

09/11/06	*Jackson Sun* "Nashville Symphony moves into new orchestra hall"	Schermerhorn Symphony Center

09/11/06   *Gramophone Magazine*   Schermerhorn Symphony
"Nashville's new hall: a triumph"   Center

09/10/06   *The Tennessean*   Schermerhorn Symphony
BRAVO!   Center
"Sumptuous gala celebrates opening of
symphony center"
"Elite crowd fills audience"
"City's musical elite step out for gala"
"Audience at gala opening says event is
'like the Oscars or the Emmys'"
"Musicians tune up in comfort in hall's
spacious backstage"
"Symphony gives dazzling concert"
"Intriguing sound calls symphony crowd
back from intermission"
A STRIKING COMPOSITION:
"$123.5 million world-class music center
sets stage for Symphony's new era"

09/10/06   *Adaptistration*   Schermerhorn Symphony
"Nashville Symphony Gala Review"   Center

09/07/06   ArchNewsNow.com   Schermerhorn Symphony
"INSIGHT: Sounding Good: 'Inspired by the   Center
classics, the acoustician for Nashville's new
Schermerhorn Symphony Center explains how
architecture and acoustics take a concert hall
into the future'"

09/05/06   Associated Press   Schermerhorn Symphony
"New Nashville Hall: Classical and Country"   Center

09/03/06   *New York Times*   Schermerhorn Symphony
"This Season's Must-Have Urban Accessory: Center
'Every city that's any city has one, but are fancy new
concert halls as good as they sound?'"
"In Cities Across the United States,
It's Raining Concert Halls"
"New Halls, by the Numbers"

09/03/06	*Atlanta Journal-Constitution* "Nashville has hall; Atlanta, big plans"	Schermerhorn Symphony Center
Sep. '06	*AT HOME Tennessee Magazine* "An Overture for a New Era: 'The new Schermerhorn Symphony Center is a masterful addition to downtown Nashville'"	Schermerhorn Symphony Center
Sep. '06	*Contract Magazine* "pomp and circumstance 'Today's performing arts centers celebrate democracy and community with designers that are as important as the performances themselves'"	Performing Arts Centers David Schwarz
Aug. '06	*Building Design & Construction Magazine* "Rightsizing Performing Arts Venues"	Schermerhorn Symphony Center
07/14/06	*Spartanburg Herald-Journal* "Arts group draws up search committee"	Chapman Cultural Center
07/05/06	*New York Times* "Anna Lee Aldred, 85, Hall of Fame Cowgirl"	National Cowgirl Museum and Hall of Fame
06/29/06	*The Tennessean* "Symphony salutes its builders"	Schermerhorn Symphony Center
06/25/06	*Las Vegas SUN* "The Vision"; "the work"; "Smith Center won't be cheap"	The Smith Center for the Performing Arts
06/22/06	*Wall Street Journal* "Fort Worth's Center City Market Sees a Texas-Sized Rebound"	Sundance Square
06/21/06	*Dallas Morning News* "Uptown's Victory in the making"	American Airlines Center
06/21/06	*Washington Post* "Phyllis Lambert Awarded Scully Prize"	Scully Prize
06/11/06	*Memphis Commercial Appeal* "Classical acts"	Schermerhorn Symphony Center
05/28/06	*New York Times* "Going to Nashville"	Schermerhorn Symphony Center

05/20/06   *Spartanburg Herald-Journal*   Chapman Cultural Center
"Topping-out party"

04/28/06   *Spartanburg Herald-Journal*   Chapman Cultural Center
"Cultural center a big winner in state budget"

Mar./Apr. '06   ARCHI-TECH   American Airlines Center
"Slam Dunk; 'American Airlines Center scores
winning digital signage'"
"A Victory for Signage"

03/20/06   *Fort Worth Star-Telegram*   Southlake Town Square
"Everyone's Town Square"

03/11/06   *Spartanburg Herald-Journal*   Chapman Cultural Center
"Center taking shape"

01/28/06   *Spartanburg Herald-Journal*   Chapman Cultural Center
"Arts Partnership exceeds fundraising goals
by $10,000"

01/21/06   *Washington Post*   Scully Prize/David Schwarz
"Phyllis Lambert Awarded Scully Prize"

12/18/05   *The Tennessean*   Schermerhorn Symphony
"Symphony Center façade comes alive with   Center
the sight of music"

10/30/05   *Indianapolis Star*   Carmel Regional Performing
"A building for people"   Arts Center

10/26/05   *Washington Post*   Scully Prize/David Schwarz
"Prince Charles to Accept Scully Prize
at Building Museum"

10/23/05   *Spartanburg Herald-Journal*   Chapman Cultural Center
"Creating Common Ground"

10/21/05   *Spartanburg Herald-Journal*   Chapman Cultural Center
"Cultural center design has downtown in mind"

10/19/05   *Spartanburg Herald-Journal*   Chapman Cultural Center
"Center delights donors"

10/19/05   *Spartanburg Herald-Journal*   Chapman Cultural Center
"Unveiling a Masterpiece: 'Center delights donors'"

10/10/05	*Contract Magazine* "Nearing Completion in Nashville"	Schermerhorn Symphony Symphony Center
10/08/05	*Dallas Morning News* "Beholding Firewheel and rain" "Garland: Chill didn't keep crowd from hottest opening in town"	Firewheel Town Center
10/07/05	*Dallas Morning News* "Firewheel gets rolling today" "Garland: Leaders are thrilled at what mall brings to suburbs"	Firewheel Town Center
10/06/05	*Dallas Morning News* "After years of negotiations, Firewheel mall to open"	Firewheel Town Center
Sep. '05	*DFW Construction News* "Gilbane completes Tarrant County Family Law Center	Tarrant County Family Law Center
08/23/05	*Indianapolis Star* "Architect chosen to design art center"	Carmel Regional Performing Arts Center
June/July '05	*AIA/DC News* Member News	Sid Richardson Collection
06/29/05	*Memphis Commercial Appeal* "Hospital's plan will make it easier to lure top team, experts say"	Le Bonheur Children's Medical Center
06/28/05	*Memphis Commercial Appeal* "$235 million project would include 12-story tower"	Le Bonheur Children's Medical Center
06/10/05	*Wall Street Journal* "Minor Pleasures"	Dr Pepper / 7Up Ballpark
May/June '05	*AIA/DC News* Member News Firewheel Town Center	Schermerhorn Symphony Center
05/22/05	*Spartanburg Herald-Journal* "What happens when community leaders meet with Texans"	Chapman Cultural Center

Feb. '05	GlobeSt.RETAIL "Sundance Square's a CBD Hit"	Sundance Square	213
04/19/05	*Washington Post* "Kenneth Schermerhorn; Nashville Symphony Leader	Schermerhorn Symphony Center	
04/01/05	*American Way* "TEXAS" and Hall of Fame	Bass Performance Hall National Cowgirl Museum	
02/23/05	*Washington Post* "Architects Offer Bids for Nats' Stadium"	Washington Nationals Baseball Stadium	
01/27/05	*Fort Worth Star-Telegram* "Architect designed local landmarks"	Philip Johnson Obituary	
01/16/05	*Spartanburg Herald-Journal* "Firm picked to design arts center"	Chapman Cultural Center	
Jan. '05	*Architectural Record* "Beating the Odds"	Schermerhorn Symphony Center	
Winter/2004	New Towns "Fort Worth Texas: New Urbanism with a Texas Twang"	Sundance Square	
10/25/04	*The Tennessean* "It's all about the sound"	Schermerhorn Symphony Center	
Oct. '04	*AIA/DC News* Member News Campus Master Plan	Chapman Cultural Center Duke University Central	
Aug. '04	BASEBALLPARKS.COM "Best New Ballpark for 2003"	Dr Pepper/7Up Ballpark	
07/27/04	*Spartanburg Herald-Journal* "Council to update master plan" CHANGES: "City to negotiate agreement with Architect who designed cultural center"	Renaissance Park	
07/21/04	*Duke University Chronicle* "Duke lays the tracks for Grand Central"	Duke University Central Campus	

06/25/04	*New York Times* "JOURNEYS; 36 Hours / Fort Worth	Sundance Square National Cowgirl Museum and Hall of Fame Sid Richardson Collection
05/07/04	*Dallas Business Journal* "Ameriquest acquires naming rights to Ballpark in Arlington	Ballpark in Arlington
04/22/04	*Dallas Observer* "Perfect Town, USA"	Parker Square Frisco Square Southlake Town Center
04/01/04	*Retail Traffic* "I Want to be a Cowgirl"	National Cowgirl Museum and Hall of Fame
Mar./Apr. '04	*Traditional Building* "A Traditionalist Comes of Age"	Firm Monograph
01/09/04	*Dallas Business Journal* "Fort Worth science museum hires Disney veteran"	National Cowgirl Museum and Hall of Fame Western Heritage Plaza
01/04/04	*Washington Post* Travel: Fort Worth, Tex	National Cowgirl Museum and Hall of Fame
Jan./Feb. '04	*Traditional Building* "Neoclassicism Texas-Style"	Fort Worth Central Library
12/15/03	Entertainment Design Online "Nashville Symphony Groundbreaking Ceremony	Schermerhorn Symphony Center
12/04/03	*Nashville Symphony In the Loop* "Schermerhorn and the Nashville Symphony Orchestra Receive Grammy Nomination"	Schermerhorn Symphony Center
12/03/03	*Nashville Symphony In the Loop* "Nashville Symphony Breaks Ground for World-Class Concert Hall"	Schermerhorn Symphony Center
12/03/03	*The Tennessean* "Ground broken for work on $120 million symphony hall"	Schermerhorn Symphony Center
Dec. '03	*Dallas-Ft. Worth Construction News* Linbeck's teamwork brightens facility	Cook Children's Medical Center

Nov. '03	*AIArchitect* "AIA Fort Worth Honors Seven Projects In the Great State of Texas"	Dr Pepper/7Up Ballpark Bass Performance Hall
10/26/03	*Wine Spectator* "The Entrepreneur and the Ambassador"	Private Residence Napa Valley
10/17/03	*Fort Worth-Star Telegram* "Kids Hospitals Grow Up—'Cook Children's opening patient pavilion as demand for such facilities increases nationwide'"	Cook Children's Medical Center
10/06/03	*Forbes Magazine Special Issue* "Building Relationships"	DMS Sundance West Bass Performance Hall
Oct. '03	*AIA/DC News* Member News	Firewheel Town Center
Oct. '03	*Architectural Record* "Great Buildings Deserve Deco Doors"	Severance Hall
09/02/03	*Wall Street Journal* "L'Enfant Terrible: New Plan Orphans Kennedy Center"	DMS/Kennedy Center
Sep. '03	Washington Building Congress *Bulletin* "DMS/AS selected as the design architect for Firewheel Town Center in Garland, TX"	Firewheel Town Center
08/25/03	*New York Times* "Connie Reeves, a Cowgirl Until the End, Dies at 101"	National Cowgirl Museum and Hall of Fame
Aug. '03	*Southern Living* "Calling all Cowgirls"	National Cowgirl Museum and Hall of Fame
July/Aug. '03	Washington Building Congress *Bulletin* Member Projects	Dr Pepper/7 Up Ballpark
06/25/03	*New York Times* "Finally, a Ballpark Gets a Neighbor" Dr Pepper/7Up Ballpark American Airlines Center	Ballpark in Arlington and Master Plan

Summer '03	*The Line—The Masonry Magazine of Texas* "Dallas Cast Stone—A Tradition of Integrity	Bank One Building National Cowgirl Museum and Hall of Fame
06/12/03	*Duke University Chronicle* "Let the designing begin…"	Duke University Central Campus
06/03/03	*Texas Construction* "Top Texas Projects"/Named #1	Dr Pepper/7Up Ballpark
06/01/03	*New York Times* "Organs Roar Back, All Pipes Blaring"	Severance Hall
June '03	*Official Visitor's Guide to Fort Worth, Texas* "The Real City of Angels"	Bass Performance Hall National Cowgirl Museum and Hall of Fame Sundance Square The Ballpark in Arlington Sid Richardson Collection
05/18/03	Joe Mock's BASEBALLPARKS.COM "Named for soda pop, but with a champagne design"	Dr Pepper/7Up Ballpark
05/11/03	*New York Times* "Fort Worth Updates Its Museums"	National Cowgirl Museum and Hall of Fame
04/04/03	*Wall Street Journal* "The Irresistible Hall of Fame"	National Cowgirl Museum and Hall of Fame
04/04/03	*Dallas Morning News* "Eager fans pack Frisco ballpark" "Sellout crowd soaks up the atmosphere in RoughRiders opener	Dr Pepper/7Up Ballpark
04/04/03	Texas Cable News Notebook: "New ballpark stands up to scrutiny" "RoughRiders' new stadium impresses major leaguer"	Dr Pepper/7Up Ballpark
04/03/03	Texas Cable News "Ballpark reviews: Fans like what they already see" Editorial: Home Run "New ballpark will help define the community"	Dr Pepper/7Up Ballpark
04/03/03	*Dallas Morning News* "Frisco swings for the fences with new stadiums"	Dr Pepper/7Up Ballpark

03/31/03	Texas Cable News "Frisco fans enjoy glimpse of ballpark"	Dr Pepper/7Up Ballpark
03/10/03	Press Release "New Ballpark Opening Day Set for April 3rd, 2003 In Frisco, Texas"	Dr Pepper/7Up Ballpark
03/03/03	*Engineering News Record* "Nashville Symphony unveiled the design for a $120-million world-class concert hall"	Schermerhorn Symphony Center
Mar. '03	*Architecture* "Survey says…Neoclassical"	Schermerhon Symphony Center
02/21/03	*In the Loop*—Newsletter of the Nashville Symphony Hall Concert Project "Nashville Symphony Board Names New Concert Hall Building for Kenneth Schermerhorn"	Schermerhorn Symphony Center
02/15/03	*Fort Worth Star-Telegram* "Congressman criticizes museum appropriations"	National Cowgirl Museum and Hall of Fame
01/22/03	*Dallas Morning News* "Local firms sponsor Frisco ballpark—RoughRiders deal goes to Dr Pepper/Seven Up and Dr Pepper Bottling	Dr Pepper/7Up Ballpark
2003	*Medicine Moves to the Mall* David Charles Sloan & Beverlie Conant Sloane	Cook Children's Medical Center
Oct. '02	*Stone World* "Limestone communicates cowgirl spirit"	National Cowgirl Museum and Hall of Fame
Oct. '02	*Cowboys and Indians* "Spirt of the Cowgirl: 'The Story of Winning the West is proudly presented in Fort Worth'"	National Cowgirl Museum and Hall of Fame
Fall '02	*Design Solutions* "Spirit of the Cowgirl Spurs Exciting Museum Design"	National Cowgirl Museum and Hall of Fame
2002	*David M. Schwarz / Architectural Services 1976–2001* Grayson Publishing	David M. Schwarz / Architectural Services
2002	*Interior Spaces of the USA and Canada* The Images Publishing Group Pty Ltd	Southlake Town Hall Sundance 11-AMC Cinemas Bass Performance Hall

2002	*Ohio Construction Review* Commercial & Retail Development/Northern Ohio	Severance Hall
12/16-22/02	*AIArchitect* "Music City, USA, Plans 'Best Symphony Hall in the World'"	Schermerhorn Symphony Center
11/20/02	*The Tennessean* "Symphony hall evokes 'Athens of the South'" "Music hall aspires to 'timeless' design" "Design critiques: 'appropriate,' 'disturbing', 'interesting mix'"	Schermerhorn Symphony Center
11/19/02	*The Tennessean* "Symphony hall plans go classic"	Schermerhorn Symphony Center
11/12/02	*TexasArchitect*	West Village
10/31/02	*Fort Worth Star-Telegram* "Construction to start on family court building"	Tarrant County Family Law Center
10/19/02	*The Tennessean* "Music to your ears—'The key to the symphony's future concert hall: blending art and science in Paul Scarbrough in perfect harmony'"	Schermerhorn Symphony Center
Sep./Oct. '02	*Preservation* "They built this City—'The Work of Architects Walker & Weeks tells the story of Cleveland's Coming of Age'"	Severance Hall
09/01/02	*The Tennessean* "As we await the new hall, our patience will be tested"	Schermerhorn Symphony Center
Summer '02	*BOMA—Tarrant Points West Magazine* "National Cowgirl Museum and Hall of Fame opened to critical acclaim"	National Cowgirl Museum and Hall of Fame
08/17/02	*The Tennessean* "The music hall man"	Schermerhorn Symphony Center
July/Aug. '02	*Southern Building Magazine* Magazine Cover	Bass Performance Hall

07/21/02	*Fort Worth-Star Telegram* "Building anticipation: Planners say new $250 million arts complex in Dallas will fill the seats and the street outside"	Bass Performance Hall
06/14-20/02	*Dallas Business Journal* "New Bank One offers stark contrast to old"	Bank One Building
06/13/02	*Wall Street Journal* "Even Cowgirls get their due"	National Cowgirl Museum and Hall of Fame
06/09/02	*Fort Worth Star-Telegram* "Retro Fight—'Architect David Schwarz is remaking Fort Worth in a resplendent, nostalgic style. But some critics find his historicism too contrived'"	David Schwarz
06/09/02	*Fort Worth Star-Telegram* "Cowgirls on parade" "Life at a gallop—'A portrait gallery of six honorees in the Cowgirl Hall of Fame'"	National Cowgirl Museum and Hall of Fame
06/09/02	*Fort Worth Star-Telegram* "Town Square can still become a true downtown"	Southlake Town Square
06/08/02	*Fort Worth Star-Telegram* "For the cowgirls—'New building for old dream to honor spirit inductees'"	National Cowgirl Museum and Hall of Fame
06/07/02	*Fort Worth Star-Telegram* "West's Best—'A new facility pays tribute to a can-do spirit'" "Justice O'Connor joins Cowgirl Museum fete"	National Cowgirl Museum and Hall of Fame
06/02/02	*Fort Worth Star-Telegram* "The Westerner—'Justice Sandra Day O'Connor talks about her life as a cowgirl'" "Wild West Women—'Saddle up to enjoy tributes, style and history at the National Cowgirl Museum and Hall of Fame'" "Museum's top wranglers" "Artist's mural brings cowgirls to life" "10 cool things at the Cowgirl Museum" "Cowgirl palace"	National Cowgirl Museum and Hall of Fame
06/02/02	*New York Times* "Where Cowgirls go to get their due"	National Cowgirl Museum and Hall of Fame

05/19/02	*Hartford Courant*
	"Gothic Harmony: 'Yale's Environmental
	Science Center Stands Out by Fitting in'"
		Yale Class of 1954
		  Environmental Science
		  Center

May '02	*Yale Alumni Magazine*
	"Designed for Science"
		Yale Class of 1954
		  Environmental Science
		  Center

04/11-17/02	*Nashville Scene* "Best advice for Symphony Hall designer David Schwarz: Respect the site"	Schermerhorn Symphony Center
04/05/02	*Fort Worth Star Telegram* Boomtown—"The Ballpark is a natural at producing homers, hits"	Ballpark in Arlington
Apr. '02	*Masonry Construction* "Patterns Elegance"	West Village
03/25/02	*Dallas Morning News* "Sound benefits—Unsung Maddox-Muse venues complement Fort Worth's Bass Hall"	Maddox-Muse Center
02/06/02	*The Tennessean* "Symphony picks Fourth Avenue South fire station to call home"	Schermerhorn Symphony Center
02/05/02	*Texas Construction*—Best Projects of 2001 "Best of 2001 Judges' Award"	American Airlines Center
Feb. '02	*Masonry Construction* "Masonry construction's project of the year"	American Airlines Center
Jan. '02	*The InTowner* "Tivoli developer gets nod as lead in partnership for Wax Museum site"	Mount Vernon Walk
Winter '02	*BOMA: Tarrant points west* "Interview with Ed Bass"	Sundance Square Masterplan

Winter '02	*Yale Environmental News*
	"Yale dedicates Class of '54
	Environmental Science Center"
		Yale Class of 1954
		  Environmental Science
		  Center

2002	*2002 Ohio Construction Review* "Concept to Completion"	Severance Hall

Awards

11/09/07	Society of American Registered Architects *Design Award of Merit*	Schermerhorn Symphony Center
2007	The National Sculpture Society *The Henry Hering Memorial Medal for* *collaboration between architect, sculptor and* *owner in the distinguished use of sculpture*	Nancy Lee and Perry R. Bass Performance Hall
2006	Washington Architectural Foundation CANstruction "We're not in CANsas anymore" *Honorable Mention*	David M. Schwarz / Architectural Services
2006	AIA Academy of Architecture for Justice *Certificate of Merit*	Tarrant County Family Law Center
2006	Architectural Precast Association for Design and Manufacturing Excellence *Award for Excellence*	Firewheel Town Center
Dec. '03	*Texas Construction Magazine* Best of 2003—*Sports & Entertainment* Best of 2003—*Architectural Design*	Dr Pepper/7Up Ballpark
10/16/03	American Institute of Architects Fort Worth Chapter *2003 Excellence In Architecture Award* *Award of Merit*	Dr Pepper/7Up Ballpark
10/16/03	American Institute of Architects Fort Worth Chapter *2003 Excellence In Architecture Award* *Citation Award*	Nancy Lee and Perry R. Bass Performance Hall
10/01/03	Society of American Registered Architects *Design Award of Merit*	American Airlines Center
10/01/03	Society of American Registered Architects *Design Award of Merit*	Yale Class of 1954 Environmental Science Center
10/01/03	Society of American Registered Architects *Design Award for Excellence*	Dr Pepper / 7Up Ballpark
06/01/03	*Texas Construction Magazine* *#1 Top Texas Projects of 2003*	Dr Pepper / 7Up Ballpark

05/31/03	Society of American Registered Architects California Council *Design Award for Excellence*	American Airlines Center
05/31/03	Society of American Registered Architects California Council *Design Award of Merit*	Parker Square Master Plan

05/31/03	Society of American Registered Architects
	California Council
	Design Award of Honor
		Yale Class of 1954
		   Environmental Science
		   Center

11/15/02	The Architectural Woodwork Institute *Award of Excellence*	National Cowgirl Museum and Hall of Fame
11/08/02	Athletic Business Magazine Twenty-Second Annual Facilities of Merit *2002 Facility of Merit Award*	American Airlines Center
10/25/02	Society of American Registered Architects *Design Award of Honorable Mention*	Bank One Building

08/17/02	International Masonry Institute
	New England Regional Golden Trowel Awards
	Achievement in Architectural Design, Construction,
	and Craftmanship in Masonry
	Outstanding Use of Masonry
		Yale Class of 1954
		   Environmental Science
		   Center

May '02	United Masonry Contractors Association Golden Trowel Award *Outstanding Architectural Design* *Brick Winner*	American Airlines Center
May '02	United Masonry Contractors Association Golden Trowel Award *Outstanding Architectural Design* *Residential & Other Winner*	West Village
03/12/02	American Council of Engineering Companies Honor Award—Structural Engineering Walter P. Moore *Best Engineering Project in the Nation for 2001*	American Airlines Center
04/06/02	American Council of Engineering Companies Highest Honor—The Eminent Conceptor Award Walter P. Moore *Most Outstanding Project in the Nation for 2001*	American Airlines Center

03/05/02	Association of General Contractors of Texas Summit Award *2001 Outstanding Project Over $30m*	American Airlines Center
Mar. '02	*Texas Construction Magazine* *Best of 2001 Judges Award*	American Airlines Center
02/27/02	Subcontractors Association of North Texas *2001 Outstanding Project Over $25m* and *Outstanding Project Team*	American Airlines Center
10/19/01	Society of American Registered Architects National Professional Design Awards Program *Design of Honor Award for Recognition of Superior* *Achievement & Professional Design Excellence*	Maddox Muse Center
10/18/01	National Trust for Historic Preservation National Preservation Award *For the sensitive restoration and expansion of* *Severance Hall, the world-famous home of the* *Cleveland Orchestra*	Severance Hall
05/08/01	United Masonry Contractors Association *Golden Trowel Award for Outstanding* *Craftsmanship in Residential and Other*	Southlake Town Hall
2001	National Terrazo & Mosaic Association *Honor Award*	American Airlines Center
2001	United States Institute for Theatre Technology, Inc. (USITT) *Honor Award*	Severance Hall
11/17/00	American Institute of Architects Washington Chapter *Merit Award for Outstanding Achievement* *In Historic Resources*	Severance Hall
10/20/00	Society of American Registered Architects National Design Awards *Award of Excellence—Gold Ribbon*	Severance Hall
Oct. '00	Associated Masonry Contractors of Houston *2000 Golden Trowel Award*	Maddox Muse Center

Sep. '00	American Institute of Architects Washington Chapter *Award of Merit* *In Historical Resources*	Severance Hall
Summer '00	The Texas Masonry Council *2000 Golden Trowel Regional Award* *for design elements and craftsmanship*	Maddox Muse Center
July '00	The Cleveland Restoration Society 2000 Preservation Award *Trustee Honor Award for Presentation Achievement*	Severance Hall
05/25/00	American Institute of Architects Cleveland Chapter *Certificate in Recognition of Exceptional* *Accomplishment in Areas of Preservation,* *Restoration, Adaptive Re-use and Maintenance* *of an Architecturally Significant Building*	Severance Hall
04/29/00	Society of American Registered Architects California Council *Design Award for Excellence*	Southlake Town Square
04/29/00	Society of American Registered Architects California Council *Design Award for Excellence*	Severance Hall
May '99	The Chicago Athenaeum: Museum of Architecture and Design *The American Architecture Awards Program, 1999*	Bass Performance Hall
Mar. '99	Masonry Contractors Association of America (Education/Government Category) Presented to LUCIA for exterior stonework *International Excellence in Masonry*	Bass Performance Hall
Mar. '99	American Institute of Steel Construction Engineering Awards of Excellence *Award of Merit*	Bass Performance Hall
03/04/99	*Texas Architect Magazine* American Institute of Architects—Ft. Worth Chapter *Award of Merit*	Disney's Wide World of Sports
Jan. '99	Associated Builders and Contractors *1998 Excellence in Construction* *First Place*	Bass Performance Hall

Dec. '98/ Jan. '99	*Holiday/Travel Magazine* *Travel Holidays 1999 Insider Awards*	Bass Performance Hall
10/24/97	Society of American Registered Architects *Design Award of Honor*	Sundance East
1997	United Masonry Contractors *1997 Golden Trowel Award* *Outstanding Brick Design*	Sundance East
Nov. '96	Society of American Registered Architects *Award of Merit*	Worthington Hotel Renovation
10/25/96	Society of American Registered Architects *Design Award of Merit*	Worthington Hotel Renovation
02/06/95	American Institute of Architects Fort Worth Chapter *Certificate of Achievement*	Worthington Hotel Renovation
Feb. '95	Associated Builders and Contractors *First Place—Excellence in* *Construction awards competition*	Ballpark in Arlington
1995	Historic Preservation Council for Tarrant County, Texas *1995 Historic and Cultural Landmarks* *Commission Award*	Sanger Lofts
11/19/94	American Institute of Architects Fort Worth Chapter *Certificate of Recognition for Creating a Notable* *Urban Experience in a Civic Center Piece*	Ballpark in Arlington
10/21/94	Society of American Registered Architects *Design Award of Merit*	Sundance West
10/21/94	Society of American Registered Architects *Design Excellence*	Ballpark in Arlington
1994	Dallas Business Journal Real Estate Awards *Best Community Impact-Architectural*	Ballpark in Arlington
03/15/93	Associated Builders and Contractors *Excellence in Construction* *Award of Merit*	Sundance Cinemas

1993	Associated Builders and Contractors *Outstanding Achievement* *Excellence in Construction*	Sundance Cinemas
1993	Illuminating Engineering Society International Illumination Design Awards *Edwin F. Guth Memorial Lighting* *Award of Excellence*	Sundance Cinemas
11/06/92	American Institute of Architects D.C. Chapter *Design Excellence*	Sundance Cinemas
11/06/92	Society of American Registered Architects *Design Award of Merit*	Sundance Cinemas
11/06/92	American Institute of Architects D.C. Chapter *Award for Excellence*	Sundance Cinemas
July '92	Building Owners and Managers Association *In Pursuit of Excellence:* *Building of the Year Award*	Cook Children's Medical Center
1991	Society of American Registered Architects *Professional Design Awards Program*	1133 Connecticut Avenue Cook Children's Medical Center The Saratoga
1991	Texas Rangers Ballpark Design *Competition—Contract Award*	Ballpark in Arlington
1990	Associated General Contractors of America Fort Worth Chapter *Outstanding Building Projects Award*	Cook Children's Medical Center
1990	Landscape Contractors Association *Grand Award—Environmental Landscape* *Award*	Private Residence
1990	American Institute of Architects Architecture for Housing *Design for Living Design Award*	The Saratoga
1990	*Interiors* Washington Design Celebration *Competition—Design Award*	Design for a Wedding

1989	The Masonry Institute	The Saratoga
	Special Achievement Design Award	
1988	Landscape Contractors Association	Private Residence
	Merit Award	
	Environmental Landscape Award	
1988	Landscape Contractors Association	Merrywood
	DCA Landscape Architects, Inc.	
	Environmental Landscape Award	
1988	The Masonry Institute	1133 Connecticut Avenue
	Special Achievement Design Award	
1987	The Masonry Institute	Penn Theater Project
	Design Award	
1986	*Mayor's Architectural Design Awards*	"Downtown Stages" Theater Study
1985	The Masonry Institute	1818 N Street
	Design Award	
1984	Art Deco Society of Washington	Penn Theater Project
	First Annual Preservation Award	
1984	The Masonry Institute	1718 Connecticut Avenue
	Design Award	

Selected Lectures &
Exhibitions of Work

06/13/07   The Institute of Classical Architecture & Classical America—The Fellows' Summer Lecture
Series *Historic Cities in Transition*. New York School of Interior Design; New York, NY.
"The Current Classical Revival in Nashville"
Lecture

03/29/07   Andrews University
Berrien Springs, Michigan
"The Process of the Work of David M. Schwarz / Architectural Services"
Lecture

09/06/06   The Institute of Classical Architecture & Classical America—Tennessee Chapter
Nashville, Tennessee
"Context and Classicism in the Creation of the Schermerhorn Symphony Center"
Lecture and tour of Schermerhorn Symphony Center

07/18/06   American Institute of Architects
Washington, D.C.
"Mixed-use Projects: Bringing together life, work, and play"
Lecture

02/03/05   The Collegiate School
New York, New York
Presentation overview of architecture and David M. Schwarz / Architectural Services to 2nd Grade Class

09/29/03   Chicago Architecture Foundation and the Clio Society of Northwestern University
Chicago, Illinois
Symposium: Taking the Field—The Future of Sports Architecture

06/24/03   Institute for Traditional Architecture/Classical Council
Alexandria, Virginia
"Class of 1954 Environmental Sciences Center, Yale University"

06/20/03   Congress For New Urbanism
Washington, D.C.
"Urban Buildings: Creativity and self-expression within contextual constraints"

03/10/03   National Building Museum
Washington, D.C.
"The Origins of Style"
Lecture and Book Signing

09/17/02   University of Miami/School of Architecture
Coral Gables, Florida
"The Origins of Style"
Lecture

04/18/02   92ⁿᵈ Street Y
New York, New York
"Knitting Together Old and New: What if Modernism Never Happened?"
Lecture

01/16/02   Case Western Reserve University—Weatherhead School of Management
Cleveland, Ohio
"Art and Management can be learned from each other"
Lecture on the renovation and expansion of Severance Hall
With Tom Morris, Executive Director of Severance Hall

09/01/01   American Institute of Architects (AIA)
Design in Historic Preservation
Old Town Alexandria, Virginia/Washington, D.C.
"Design Issues in Classical Architecture"
Lecture on the philosophical approach to the renovations at
Severance Hall

03/31/01   Congress on New Urbanism
Charleston, South Carolina
"Southlake Town Square"
Lecture

03/29/00   Cleveland Club of Washington
Washington, D.C.
"Restoration of Severance Hall"
Lecutre: Craig P. Williams, Project Architect, and
Gary Hanson, Executive Associate Director of Severance Hall

03/23/00   University of Notre Dame
Notre Dame, Indiana
"What if Modernism Never Happened?"
Lecture

01/07/00   Hawken School
Gates Mills, Ohio
"The Expansion and Renovation of Severance Hall as an example of
Architectural and Visual Literacy as it relates to our daily lives"
Upper School & Faculty Lecture

10/25/99   Yale University
New Haven, Connecticut
"Environmental Diversity: A Discussion of Style and Context in Architecture"
Lecture

10/19/99	Partners for Livable Communities National Conference "Crossing the Line" Memphis, Tennessee Panel Chairman: "Downtown Investment Strategies—Revitalizing the Core"
09/23/99	Greater Dallas Planning Council Dallas, Texas "Building Better Cities" Lecture
06/07– 08/16/99	The American Architecture Awards "New Architecture Designed in the United States" The Chicago Athenaeum/Museum of Architecture and Design, Chicago, Illinois (Exhibit—Nancy Lee and Perry R. Bass Performance Hall)
04/11/99	Yale Constructs Symposium Yale University School of Architecture; New Haven, Connecticut Presentation of Yale University Environmental Science Center
10/23/98	Society of American Registered Architects National Convention Washington, D.C. "The Roots of the Reds: Washington's Architectural Heritage" Lecture
10/08/98	Urban Land Institute Dallas, Texas "The Economics of Architecture" Lecture
09/15/98	National Building Museum *(Architects of Downtown Cultural Series)* "Building Culture Downtown: New Ways of Revitalizing the American City" Lecture
05/01- 01/03/99	National Building Museum Washington, D.C. "Building Culture Downtown: New Ways of Revitalizing the American City" (Exhibit: Nancy Lee and Perry R. Bass Performance Hall)
11/19/97	Texas Tech University Lubbock, Texas College of Architecture "New Life for the American Downtown"
05/01/96	Virgin Cinemas "Theaters and Cinemas"

02/03/96	University of Texas Austin, Texas School of Architecture "Compilation of David M. Schwarz Architectural Services Projects"
10/17/95	City Planning Association "Relations between the Private and Public Sectors"
10/14/95	American Planning Association "Planning for Entertainment—If you Build, Will They Come?"
Sep. '93	Traveling Exhibit: "Field of Dreams: Architecture and Baseball"
05/13/93	Dallas Museum of Art Dallas, Texas "Texas Rangers Ballpark"
04/06/93	Modern Art Museum of Fort Worth Fort Worth, Texas "Toward the Next New Architecture or When Cathedrals Weren't White"
03/27/93	Trilateral Commission "The Embassies of Kalaroma"
03/25/92	The Washington Design Center "Texas Rangers Ballpark and Other Works in Progress"
05/17/91	A.I.A. National Convention "Current Residential Design"
Oct./Nov. '90	National Building Museum/Washington Chapter A.I.A. "Give Us your Best," (Exhibition and Catalogue)
06/21/90	The Urban Land Institute "The Real Estate Development Process: New Trends in Architecture"
05/04/90	National Building Museum Tour of "Washington's Twelve Best New Office Buildings" with James M. Goode
Apr. '90	The Washington Design Center Winner of The Washington Design Celebration Competition—Exhibition

04/17/90	D.C. Preservation League Fifth Annual Gerald D. Hines interest lecture series "Preservation: The Architect's Challenge"
01/25/90	The Smithsonian Institution/National Trust for Historic Preservation "New vs. Old Design: Creating compatible architecture in Washington's historic context"
09/27/88	The Washington Design Center "Washington Today: Architecture & the City" Seminar
03/04/88	The Athenaeum "A Decade of Washington Architecture" Exhibition including The Penn Theater Project and 1818 N Street
02/18/87	The Washington Design Center "Contextual Buildings"
09/20/86	McIntosh/Drysdale Gallery Exhibition of Drawings & Models
11/13/85	The Catholic University of America Washington, D.C. "Works" Lecture & Exhibition
10/13/84	Don't Tear It Down Tour of Architects' Offices
Jan. '81	Lunn Gallery Exhibition models and drawings

Selected Commissions

2002–2008

2008

UNIVERSITY OF SOUTH CAROLINA UPSTATE BUSINESS SCHOOL
Spartanburg, South Carolina. University of South Carolina Upstate - George Dean Johnson, Jr. College of Business and Economics, Spartanburg, South Carolina. 60,000 sq. ft. Business School located downtown adjacent to the Chapman Cultural Center as part of the Renaissance Park Development. In association with McMillan Smith & Partners PLLC, Britt Peters and Associates Inc., Wade Crow Consulting Engineers, and Matrix Engineering Inc.

SOUTHLAKE OFFICE AND RETAIL BUILDING
Southlake, Texas. 25,000 sq. ft. full block footprint, two-story, office over high-end retail with three distinct façades. In association with The Beck Group.

COOK CHILDREN'S MEDICAL CENTER NORTH SHELF EXPANSION
Fort Worth, Texas. A 223,000 sq. ft. expansion of the north shelf and a new patient tower. This expansion doubles the size of the Neonatal Intensive Care Unit, includes new cafeteria and kitchen, and connects to the existing North Pavilion patient tower on all levels. In association with FKP.

COOK CHILDREN'S MEDICAL CENTER NORTH GARAGE EXPANSION AND HELIPADS
Fort Worth, Texas. A 413,000 sq. ft. expansion increases the capacity of the North Garage. The garage will be expanded to the west and increased from four to six levels of parking. Two helicopter landing pads will be located above the top parking level. In association with Intertech Design.

COOK CHILDREN'S MEDICAL CENTER MEDICAL OFFICE BUILDING
Fort Worth, Texas. A 210,000 sq. ft. medical office building will accommodate increased outpatient and laboratory services. The Medical Office Building will connect directly to the inpatient tower of the North Shelf Expansion to allow shared services and convenient communication for physicians. In association with FKP.

COOK CHILDREN'S MEDICAL CENTER SOUTH GARAGE EXPANSION
Fort Worth, Texas. A 175,000 sq. ft. expansion of the South Garage will be accomplished by adding two more parking levels above the existing four levels. In association with Conti, Jumper & Gardner.

HOTEL AND RETAIL PROJECT
Washington, D.C. 200,000 sq. ft. boutique hotel with street level retail uses near a metro station in a historic district.

COOMBS STADIUM
Durham, North Carolina. Conceptual Design for a new 5,000 seat A.C.C. Baseball Park and team facilities building designed to minor league specifications.

2007

12711 TWINBROOK PARKWAY
Twinbrook, Maryland. A 200,000 sq. ft. speculative office building representing the final phase build-out of an 800,000 sq. ft., sixteen-acre office and research and development master plan. The building's design incorporates numerous sustainable features and is targeting a LEED Gold rating.

FORT WORTH JAIL
Fort Worth, Texas. A new construction, adult detention facility located in downtown Fort Worth. The building will occupy a single city block and will connect to the County's existing jail located across the street. In association with Gideon-Toal Architects and Wiginton Hooker Jeffry Architects.

FLOWER MOUND CENTRAL BUSINESS DISTRICT MASTER PLAN
Flower Mound, Texas. Master Plan for the development of a 158-acre site near the center of Flower Mound's primary commercial area. The plan features numerous parks, squares and a central river walk surrounded by residential, office, retail, and medical uses.

440 FIRST STREET, NW
Washington, D.C. Renovation of an existing eight-story sq. ft. office building to design new skin, lobby and additional floor. In association with Inter Spec Design, Inc., Tadjer-Cohen-Edelson Associates, Inc., and META Engineers, P.C.

MASTER PLAN
Las Vegas, Nevada. Long range master plan for a casino company on the Las Vegas Strip with mixed-use development to increase overall value of holdings (uses may include upgrades of existing hotels, additional hotels and residential towers, additional retail, possible exhibit/convention center.) In association with Klai Juba Architects and WA Richardson Builders LLC.

HIGH STREET
Atlanta, Georgia. Master Plan for the redevelopment of a forty-five-acre parcel located adjacent to the Dunwoody MARTA rail station. The plan calls for 2,500 residential units, 300,000 sq. ft. of retail, 200,000 sq. ft. of hotel, and 350,000 sq. ft. of office uses. In association with Kimley-Horn and Associates.

2006

SMITH CENTER FOR THE PERFORMING ARTS
Las Vegas, Nevada. State of the art 2,055 seat multi-purpose hall, a small 600-seat theater and a cabaret theater. In association with HKS, Inc, The Whiting-Turner Contracting Company, MSA Engineering Consultants, Walter P. Moore, Fisher Dachs Associates, Akustiks, LLC, and Green Building Services.

REGENT SQUARE
Houston, Texas. Planning and partial design of a mixed-use urban development with 330,000 sq. ft. of retail and restaurant uses, 1,740 residential units, 60,000 sq. ft. of office space, and a 200-room hotel. In association with Morris Architects, Robert A.M. Stern Architects LLP, Bowie Gridley Architects, B&D Studios LLC, Aponwao Design Inc, Hartman-Cox, GRG Inc., and Haynes Whaley Associates Inc.

UNIVERSITY OF MIAMI SPACE STUDY
Coral Gables, Florida. Provisions for the addition of new buildings to the existing 265-acre Coral Gables campus over the next twenty to thirty years through a study and remapping of the overall structure of open space and pedestrian and vehicular circulation networks through and around campus.

MERRIWEATHER POST PAVILION RENOVATION
Columbia, Maryland. Site studies, planning and renovation analysis for Merriweather Post Pavilion in Columbia, Maryland.

2005

TWINBROOK OFFICE BUILDING
Twinbrook, Maryland. Design for 350,000 sq. ft., thirteen-story office building with ground floor retail.

CARNEGIE BUILDING
Fort Worth, Texas. A 280,000-sq. ft., sixteen-story Class-A office building in Sundance Square. In association with Boka Powell LLC, Blum Consulting Engineers, and Datum Engineers.

CARMEL PERFORMING ARTS CENTER
Carmel, Indiana. 1,600-seat concert hall and 500-seat multi-use theater to anchor Carmel's new mixed-use downtown development. In association with CSO Architects, Artec Consultants, Lynch, Harrison & Brumleve, and L'Acquis Consulting Engineer.

HILLVIEW MASTER PLAN
Denton, Texas. 440 acre mixed-use residential and commercial development.

NEWPORT BEACH RESORT
Port Aransas, Texas. 225,000 sq. ft. to include residential space and golf club.

2004

CHAPMAN CULTURAL CENTER
Spartanburg, South Carolina. 82,000 sq. ft. to house eight independent organizations: Art Museum, History Museum, Music Foundation, Science Center, Arts Guild, The Arts Partnership, Ballet School, and 500-seat theater. In association with Little Diversified Architectural Consulting, Linbeck Construction Company, McCracken Clopel, Michael Vergason Landscape Architects, Ltd., Creative Acoustics, and Theatre Consultants Collaborative, LLC.

LE BONHEUR CHILDRENS MEDICAL CENTER
Memphis, Tennessee. New construction of a 230-bed Children's Hospital. In association with FKP Architects, Inc., Walter P. Moore and Associates, Inc., Smith Seckman Reid, and Linbeck Construction Corporation.

1700/1800 ROCKVILLE PIKE
Rockville, Maryland. Retail and Residential development on a four-and-a-half-acre site in downtown Rockville.

PRIVATE VACATION RESIDENCE
High Desert Location. A 16,050 sq. ft. Frank Lloyd Wright style textile-block house with a pool house and a garage with an apartment above. In association with Rees Construction, Robert Silman Associates, and Beaudin Ganze Consulting Engineers Inc.

2003

VANDERBILT UNIVERSITY
Nashville, Tennessee. Master plan and conceptual design for development of 1,600-bed freshman campus on Vanderbilt's historic Peabody campus, and plans for the creation of 4,500 residential college housing units for the upper classman population on the main campus.

DUKE UNIVERSITY CENTRAL CAMPUS MASTER PLAN
Durham, North Carolina. Master plan for a 250-acre area between Duke's two historic campuses, to be developed as a new mixed-use university village, including residential, office, retail development and plans for a campus-wide transportation system. In association with Cousins Properties.

FIREWHEEL TOWN CENTER
Garland, Texas. 775,000 sq. ft. mixed-use complex located in Dallas-Ft. Worth metroplex. In association with Beck Architecture, Zinser Grossman Structural, and ARJO Engineers.

CATTLE RAISER'S MUSEUM
Fort Worth, Texas. Museum located in Ft. Worth's downtown Western Heritage Center and intended to link to the National Cowgirl Museum and Hall of Fame. In association with Gideon-Toal.

2002

MOUNT VERNON WALK
Washington, DC. Architectural design of the large, urban development won in a design competition with 11 development teams. Project includes over 500 housing units and 57,000 sq. ft. of retail. The design provides affordable and market rate housing, artists' live/work studios, a pedestrian promenade, and a live performance theater.

SCHERMERHORN SYMPHONY CENTER
Nashville, Tennessee. Design of a new construction, 1,900-seat pure concert hall for the Nashville Symphony Orchestra. In association with Earl Swenson Associates and Hastings Architecture Associates, KSI Engineers, I.C. Thomasson & Associates, Akustiks Inc., Fischer Dachs Associates, and American Constructors.

PARKWAY CENTER MASTER PLAN
Las Vegas, Nevada. Master plan for mixed-use development of a sixty-one-acre site adjacent to downtown.

PRIVATE VACATION RESIDENCE
New England. Design for a new construction private residence, guest house and pool on a beachfront estate. In association with Sourati Engineering Group and Knight/ Zadeh.

Photo Credits

Author's Note

Appearing on the 30th anniversary of David M. Schwarz Architects, this book takes me back almost as many years to when I first wrote about David, in a *Progressive Architecture* article on the "Reds," a salon of context-conscious, brick-loving young architects we helped start. Today's 50-person firm retains many aspects of that sort of forum, with David very much the creative leader. Perhaps as a result of this background, my review here of the firm's recent work is light on individual project credits. Both the firm and the author understand our responsibility to acknowledge the contributions of individual firm members, collaborators, and clients, and readers are invited to contact me at rlma@comcast.net with questions in this regard.

Many firm members gave time and thought to this book—none more so than the principals and project managers associated with the projects shown: Tom Greene (Bank One, Cook Children's Medical Center, National Cowgirl Museum); Gregory Hoss (Dr Pepper, Chapman Cultural Center); Ted House-knecht (Beringer, Hall Residence and Winery, Private Residence in New England); Michael Swartz (Firewheel, West Village, Frisco, Parker, Southlake, Tarrant County Family Law Center); and Craig Williams (Hawken, Schermer-horn Symphony Center, Sid Richardson Museum.) Rhiannon Porter and Kathryn Garrett were indefatigable in-house coordinating editors, and Ashlyn McKeithan and Jerry Marshall were among those who enabled my Texas-Nashville tour.

David Schwarz was generous with time, insight, resources, and encouragement.

Building managers and users I spoke with were helpful without exception, especially Nashville Symphony Orchestra Executive Director Alan Valentine, who gave a lucid interview and backstage tour.

The *David M. Schwarz Architects 2002-2007* monograph project team, and publisher James Trulove with the support of art directors Elizabeth Mandel and James Pittman, deserve primary credit for conceiving and realizing this book; their previous volume, *David M. Schwarz / Architectural Services 1976–2001*, was a model for this one and remains an essential guide to the firm's work.